Contents

Flying model helicopters

Dave Day

Argus Books

Argus Books
Argus House
Boundary Way
Hemel Hempstead
Hertfordshire HP2 7ST
England

ISBN 0 85242 883 9

Phototypesetting by En to En, Tunbridge Wells
Printed and bound in Great Britain by
Biddles Ltd, Guildford and King's Lynn

Introduction 1

There can be little doubt that the flying of radio controlled model helicopters is the most challenging of all the remotely controlled model flying classes. The distinction between remotely controlled models and free-flight models is deliberate since it is the writer's firm belief that certain of the free-flight competition classes offer an even greater challenge. Perhaps it should also be made clear from the outset that the term 'most challenging' does not mean that it is either the ultimate or the best – that is for the individual to decide for himself.

Those potential readers who are seeking a detailed examination of helicopter aerodynamics or a review of the current 'state-of-the-art' are strongly advised to look elsewhere since that is not the purpose of this book. Such a book would, in any case, almost certainly be out of date before it was published. What we intend to do here is to detail exactly what is entailed in the flying of model helicopters, from the early learning stage right up to competing in FAI class F3C contests. It seems highly likely that this aspect alone will sorely stretch the confines of one book.

It will, of course, be necessary to delve into some of the details of helicopter design in order to explain just how some features can be of help in the learning process. This will also be used to explain just why some highly prized extras or accessories can be safely dispensed with in the early stages!

One thing that will become increasingly clear to the budding helicopter pilot as he becomes more involved in his new hobby is the unusual degree of stratification among helicopter pilots. He will find that modeller 'A' who he regards as a capable flyer and hopes one day to emulate does, in turn, look up to 'B' who wishes that he could achieve the standards set by 'C' and so on. With a small

A *Kalt* Baron 60 EX being hovered in *very* windy conditions. Note nose down attitude. Extreme turbulence from buildings and a large crowd of spectators (out of picture) make this a situation for the very capable pilot only. Pilot Kevin Senior.

amount of perseverance our beginner can look forward to the day when someone approaches him for advice.

It is this very aspect which presents one of the major problems for those wishing to break into the hobby. Normally one would go along to some established 'name' and ask for his advice and guidance. With a few notable exceptions most of these people are now so far removed from the learning stage that they have forgotten all those little things which can give so much trouble to the newcomer.

It was this very realisation which caused the writer to embark upon writing down these things while he was still in the early stages of the learning curve. Hopefully this will assist others to avoid many of the pitfalls which can lead to time-consuming and expensive detours along the way.

For those who are having repeated problems with some little quirk of their particular model – take heart, the identical problem has probably afflicted every one of us during the learning process. If this book can serve to convince just one reader to persevere to eventual success then it will have been well worth the effort of writing it.

2   Types of helicopter

Fixed or collective pitch

All model helicopters can be divided into two basic types; those on which the pitch (or angle of incidence) of the main rotor blades is fixed and those on which the pitch can be varied.

Dealing with fixed pitch types first, we find a relatively simple, uncomplicated machine in which control of the rotor's lifting ability is effected by altering its speed via the motor's throttle control. To go up you increase power and to come down you reduce power (Figure 1). All very simple, but this very simplicity also causes one of the biggest disadvantages of this type of model. Let us assume that the model is hovering and is slowly rising. In order to stop this slow climb you close the throttle slightly which causes the main rotor to slow down. This does not happen instantly but takes a

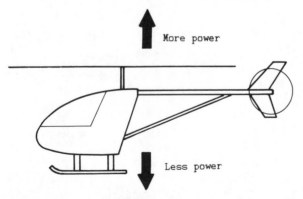

Fig. 1 Fixed pitch model uses power variation to go up or down.

measurable time to occur, during which the model continues to gain height.

When the model does stop rising, the rotor speed will probably be too slow to maintain height and the machine will now begin to descend. To stop this you must now add power. This will again take time to increase the rotor speed during which the model will descend at an increasing rate. In order to stop this descent the power will have to be increased beyond the normal hovering figure, at which point the model will begin to rise and continue to do so until the power can be reduced – which is where we came in!

The result of all this is that it is quite difficult to hover a fixed pitch machine at a constant altitude. Yes, it can be done with practice, but we are talking about beginners and practice is something they have yet to acquire. Usually the machine does a fairly good impersonation of a yo-yo – which is hardly guaranteed to inspire confidence.

One of the most difficult things for the learner helicopter pilot to master is the translation from forward to hovering flight. This manoeuvre is much more difficult with a fixed pitch model due to its inability to reduce pitch for the descent. When in forward flight, extra lift is produced by the action of the rotor disc moving through the air – rather like a frisbee. In this condition it is necessary to reduce the rotor speed to a very low level in order to reduce height, which means that control of the model is seriously impaired. It is quite normal to find that even with the throttle fully closed and the rotor blades turning at a very slow speed the model still will not lose height! Here the solution is to reduce the forward speed before attempting to lose height, which requires some proficiency and practice.

Generally, fixed pitch machines are not aerobatic and autorotations are impossible. However, the fixed pitch model helicopter is cheap, simple, easy to repair and needs less setting up than its variable pitch brother. It also has the virtue that it only requires a normal four channel radio control outfit to fly it, which is something we will explore further in a later chapter.

Collective pitch machines

Before we go any further let us explain the term 'collective pitch'. There are two ways of altering the pitch of the blades of a helicopter. In order to steer the model it is necessary to be able to alter the pitch at various points on the rotor disc. If you wish to bank to the left you would increase pitch on the right side and reduce it on the left (Figure 2). Similarly, if you wished to raise the nose you would increase pitch at the front of the disc and reduce it

The GMP *Cricket*, one of only a handful of fixed pitch helicopters available. Such machines are simpler and cost less, but have performance limitations and require more skill to fly them well.

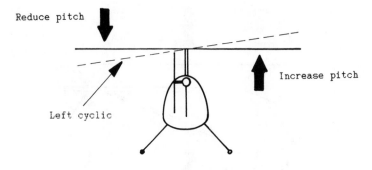

Model viewed from rear

Fig. 2 Effect of lateral cyclic pitch.

at the rear (Figure 3). This differential control of the pitch is called 'cyclic' pitch.

If you want to make the model go up or down then you would increase or reduce the pitch at all points around the rotor disc (Figure 4), hence the name 'collective' pitch. This requirement causes a considerable increase in the mechanical complexity of the machine which makes it more expensive, harder to repair and requires much more 'setting-up' to produce the best results.

Compared to the fixed pitch machines already considered the collective pitch model is easier to hover due to the response to pitch changes being virtually immediate. It is also much more versatile and capable of aerobatics and autorotations, or engine-off descents. Translation from forward to hovering flight is also much easier due to being able to reduce the blade pitch to zero or even a negative angle to aid descent.

Collective machines can be flown using a normal four channel

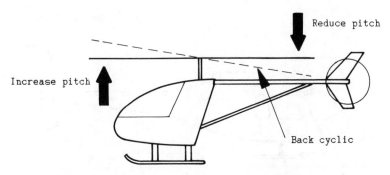

Fig. 3 Effect of fore/aft cyclic pitch.

13

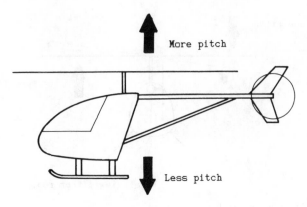

Fig. 4 Collective pitch model uses pitch variation to go up or down.

radio and this is recommended for the beginner who is unable to obtain experienced assistance.

However, to make full use of this type of machine it is necessary to use radio control equipment which is specially designed for use in helicopters. This again needs experience in setting-up and further increases the cost. The recommended procedure for those learning

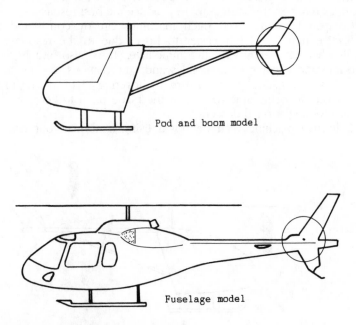

Fig. 5 Pod and boom model or fuselage type.

14

to fly on a collective pitch machine would, therefore, be to start with a normal four channel system and change this to a helicopter radio after some proficiency has been attained. This will also help to reduce the expense entailed if you should decide that choppers are not for you.

Pod and boom or fuselage

Helicopters can also be divided into those which are of pod and boom type and those which have fuselages (Figure 5). The fuselage type does not necessarily imply that the model has to be a scale model, however, since there are scale pod and boom types and also non-scale fuselage type models.

By far the largest number of models available are non-scale pod and boom types and these have much to commend them both as trainers and general sports models. They are generally cheaper, lighter, more crash resistant and easier to set-up. From this it follows that they are easier to repair and have a generally better performance. One of the commonest forms of crash damage during the learning phase lies in the rotor blades coming into contact with the tailboom. This can be difficult and expensive to repair on a fuselage model, while on a pod and boom model it can be as simple as merely straightening the boom or, at worst, replacing it. Many pod and boom type models are now designed to have a fuselage fitted at a later date so it is possible to have the best of both worlds by starting with a pod and boom model and adding a fuselage when the risk of damaging it has diminished.

Apart from the obvious feature of being better looking, fuselage type models have the great advantage that they do help considerably with the ever-present problem of orientation. By that we mean that it is easier to see just what the model is doing when it is some distance away from the pilot. The possibility of the pilot becoming disorientated and consequently making a disastrous mistake is thus reduced.

Scale models

Whether they be of the pod and boom or fuselage type, scale helicopters add still more complexity allied to greater cost and weight and increased inaccessibility. It could be said that the difference between a scale and a non-scale model is similar to the difference between a pod and boom and a fuselage type model.

However, scale models do have a charm of their own which makes the extra effort worthwhile. Nonetheless, the learner pilot would be well advised to steer well clear of the scale model until

15

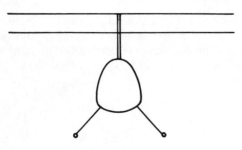

Fig. 6 Concentric rotors.

he has achieved some proficiency in flying other types of helicopter.

Aerobatic helicopters

The modern collective pitch type of helicopter equipped with a suitable radio control system and a modern high output motor is, with a suitable pilot, capable of performing any manoeuvre which can be performed by a conventional, fixed wing type of model. This degree of performance does require a specially designed model, but most sports type helicopters are capable of such basic manoeuvres as the loop and the roll.

High performance helicopter models are light, clean machines and require the most powerful motors available in order to realise their potential. Curiously enough, however, such machines are capable of being used as trainers if suitably set up by experienced hands. If experienced help is not available they should be avoided until the necessary expertise has been acquired.

This type of model does demand a specialised helicopter radio which will allow various special control options including the ability to reduce the pitch of the blades to a negative figure without closing the throttle (see later).

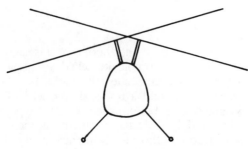

Fig. 7 Eccentric rotors.

16

Multi-rotor types

There are several multi-rotor types of helicopter currently in use in the full-size world and they have several advantages for specialist applications. However, at the time of writing such types are, in the model world, the province of experimenters only. Although the concentric rotor type (Figure 6) would, perhaps, appear to have certain advantages for our purposes, this has not been pursued to date. The eccentric rotor type (Figure 7) presents mechanical problems, while the tandem rotor (Figure 8) which is popular in the full-size world has, so far, produced control problems.

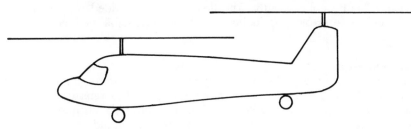

Fig. 8   Tandem rotors.

Autogyros

While superficially similar to the helicopter, the autogyro is, in fact, a quite different animal. Its rotors are, unlike the helicopter, not driven by an engine but freewheel continuously. Effectively, the autogyro is a conventional aeroplane with a rotating wing and, therefore, falls outside the scope of this book.

A salutary tale

The relative advantages of fixed versus collective pitch can be summed up by the following tale. A friend was about to test fly a new collective pitch model which was equipped with an autorotation freewheel (a device which allows the main rotor to continue to rotate at high speed after the throttle has been closed). For reasons which will become clear in later chapters the model was set up to have some negative pitch when the throttle was closed.

Unbeknown to the pilot, the pitch servo was connected in the wrong sense, i.e. closing the throttle increased the pitch and vice versa. When the throttle was opened the rotor RPM rose higher and higher without the machine showing any inclination to leave the ground. Finally, with the motor screaming its head off the throttle was sharply closed to terminate the attempt. The model promptly

17

shot up to a height of 25 feet with the blades rapidly slowing as the energy dissipated, whereupon the model began to fall. Naturally enough the owner banged the throttle wide open to arrest the fall which caused the model to literally drive itself into the ground! Fortunately the damage was not too serious.

The cheapest approach

Summing up the above remarks, we can see that the cheapest way of learning to fly model helicopters would be to start with a fixed pitch machine of the pod and boom type fitted with a standard four channel radio control outfit. The first item to be added when extra finance is available should be a tail rotor gyrostabiliser (see later).

The easiest approach

If cost is not a major consideration it would be best to start with a medium sized (0.40-0.50 cu.in. size motor) pod and boom type machine fitted with a gyrostabiliser and a standard 4/5 channel radio. If experienced help is available, the radio should be a helicopter type.

See Appendix 1 for full details of available helicopter kits.

Helicopter motors $\quad$ 3

Differences from standard types

In the earliest days of model helicopters there were, of course, no specialised helicopter motors and it was necessary to adapt engines intended for conventional fixed wing models. In a helicopter application these tended to overheat even if mounted in an exposed position in the stream of air from the rotors. An early innovation was the use of a large heatsink fitted to the cylinder head of the motor to assist with cooling. Other methods included the use of a fan fitted to the crankshaft of the motor to produce an additional flow of air. In some cases this was assisted by the use of a cooling duct to channel the air directly at the motor and this forms the basis of most modern cooling systems.

The first true helicopter motor was produced by Graupner for their *Bell 212* model. This consisted of an *HB 61* motor (essentially a German version of the American *Veco 61* engine) fitted with an additional shaft through the backplate to drive a cooling fan. A metal plate was attached to the rear of the engine which, together with a plastic moulding, formed an integral cooling duct to direct air across the cylinder head. The unit was completed by a *Perry* carburettor and a substantial flywheel. Later versions featured an enlarged cylinder head to assist further with the cooling.

This type of 'heatsink head' as it came to be called is a standard feature of all modern helicopter motors. Most manufacturers now include at least one such motor in their range. In some cases the cylinder head is the only difference from a standard motor while, in other cases, there may be several other modifications.

These can take the form of different intake and/or exhaust timing to give greater flexibility, different shaft sizes to facilitate the fitting

19

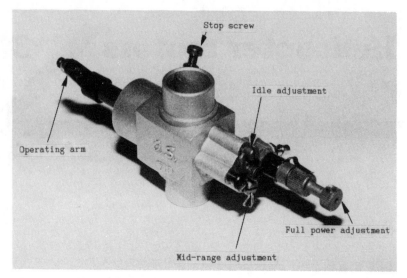

Stop screw

Idle adjustment

Operating arm

Full power adjustment

Mid-range adjustment

Fig. 9   OS 7H carburettor.

of flywheel/fan units or even non-standard carburettors. One such device is produced by the Japanese OS company (Figure 9) and has three different mixture adjustments which give independent control of the fuel/air mixture at low, mid-range and high throttle settings.

Most manufacturers also produce special silencers for their helicopter motors and an additional selection of silencers is also produced by the majority of helicopter manufacturers. A useful device is the 90° adaptor (Figure 10) which permits a standard aircraft type silencer to be rotated to suit those helicopters which mount the motor with the shaft in a vertical position.

Fig. 10   90° adaptor.

There is an exception to every rule and we should mention here a model design which is expressly intended not to use a helicopter motor. The *Star-Ranger* helicopter and its derivatives are designed and produced in Germany by Ewald Heim. These use a standard high output motor which is fitted with a very large heatsink clamped around the cylinder head. This incorporates two of the mounting points for the total mechanical package, which means that the motor itself forms the major part of the chassis and is used as a stressed member (Figure 11).

In general it can be said that the specialised helicopter motor will be heavier and more expensive than its standard counterpart. It will usually be more flexible, possibly at the expense of slightly less power. Its use may well be dictated by the design of the helicopter to which it is to be fitted.

All of the helicopter motors currently available are of the glowplug type. This means that some means of energising the plug for starting purposes is required. The vast majority of glowplugs require a 1.5 volt supply although 2 volt types are generally

Fig. 11 Heim mechanics.

available in the U.K. 1.5 volt plugs can be powered by a large capacity nickel cadmium battery if the leads are kept very short, or can be supplied from a 2 volt wet or gel cell battery by using long (about 5-6 feet) leads.

For starting purposes it will be necessary to use an electric starter. Depending on the helicopter design it will be applied via either a starting belt or a cone start device. Some cone start designs require great care in setting up if vibration is to be avoided.

Running-in

While it is possible for the experienced model helicopter flyer and/ or experienced model engine operator to run in a brand new motor in a helicopter it is highly recommended that initial running-in should be carried out on a test stand (Figure 12). This will allow any necessary adjustments to be carried out with maximum accessibility of the various controls. It will also minimise the risk of damage to the helicopter.

The first start of a new motor can sometimes be difficult and unpredictable. It is very easy to cause damage to the model under these conditions. Once the motor is running, there is a further danger of its stopping without warning which can be embarrassing if the model is some feet above the ground!

When running-in on a test stand the motor should initially be run on a propeller which is one size smaller than would normally be

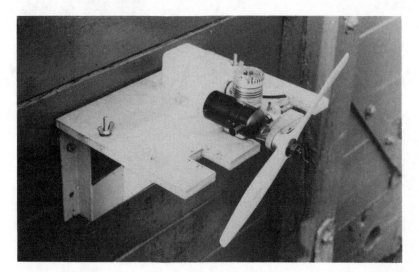

Fig. 12 Test stand.

used for that particular size of motor. This will allow the motor to be run at a normal speed on a rich mixture setting. When the motor has loosened up and will run consistently with the mixture leaned out, the idle mixture can be set up on this same propeller.

A propeller one or two sizes larger than normally recommended should then be fitted and the mixture adjusted for full throttle running. This procedure is advised even when a new motor is being run in by an experienced operator since it is extremely difficult to establish the correct setting for maximum throttle running when the motor is installed in the helicopter.

At this point let us stop a moment and explain just what is meant by the terms 'rich' and 'lean' mixture. There is one optimum value for the fuel/air ratio of the mixture which enters the motor. If the mixture contains too much fuel it is said to be 'rich' and the motor will give less power and throw unburnt fuel out of the exhaust. If insufficient fuel is supplied it is said to be a 'lean' mixture. This too will cause a loss of power and the motor will tend to overheat. If it is very lean the motor will stop.

Most modern carburettors are equipped with some means of metering the fuel supply so as to give the correct mixture during mid-range running. A situation which must be avoided in helicopters is that of setting the mid-range adjustment to compensate for an over-lean full throttle setting. Since a helicopter spends much of its time hovering – on a mid-range throttle setting – all will appear to be well until full power is needed when the motor will lose power or stop. Don't be tempted to adjust the full throttle setting by attempting to hang on to the helicopter while the motor is run up to full power. The flywheel action of the main rotor will produce a totally unexpected result to any movement of the model.

Fuels and oils

Many modern commercially available fuels contain synthetic oils in place of the traditional castor oil. While these oils are perfectly satisfactory if properly used they are much less forgiving in the event of the motor being wrongly adjusted, or if cooling is marginal. This situation is somewhat worsened if the motor is installed in a helicopter and it is strongly recommended that the fuel should contain at least some castor oil in order to give some safety margin. Many top fliers purchase fuel containing synthetic oil and then add around 5% castor oil to it.

Castor oil does give a smoky exhaust and is more difficult to clean off the model (a measure of its efficiency as a lubricant) which some people find objectionable. However, this is a small price to pay for greater reliability and ease of adjustment and the smoke can be a useful indication of wind direction!

While most glowplug motors will run quite happily on fuels consisting of just methanol and a lubricant (generally known as 'straight' fuel), it is advisable to add a small percentage – say 5% – of nitromethane. This gives considerably greater flexibility and ease of adjustment allied to an increase in power, at the cost of a slight increase in fuel consumption.

Larger percentages of nitromethane can be used if more power is required. This will be obtained at even greater expense due to higher fuel costs and greater fuel consumption. A law of diminishing returns applies here and the modeller must decide for himself just where to draw the line.

For those who wish to mix their own fuels, a good general purpose 'brew' is as follows:

Methanol	75%
Castor oil	20%
Nitromethane	5%

For running-in purposes the oil content should be increased to 25% while the methanol is reduced to 70% or the nitromethane omitted.

Never neglect the obvious

The writer's *OS 50 FSR-H* motor suffered a very serious crash as a result of which it ran at very high speed under low load until the connecting rod failed. Apart from the rod, the only damage appeared to be a dent in the piston skirt. When the rod and piston were replaced the motor ran as well as ever for a while and then began a steady decline in performance.

Since there was no obvious reason for the problem the cylinder liner and piston ring were also replaced, giving in effect a fully reconditioned engine. This did not improve the situation and the performance continued to decline. In desperation, another piston ring was fitted, again with no improvement.

Things were now reaching the point where it would have been cheaper to have bought a new motor. Another *50* size motor was, in fact, required for another helicopter so another OS *50* was purchased and fitted to the original model. There was no improvement (hands up all those who guessed) – if anything it was worse! Some thought brought the realisation that the only common denominator was the silencer and this was removed for a short (noisy) test. Needless to say the performance was now fully restored.

After soaking in cellulose thinners and much prodding with various pieces of wire a large amount of gooey black carbon was removed from the silencer and things returned to normal.

For a full list of available helicopter motors see Appendix 2.

4 Modes and trays

Mode 1 versus Mode 2 versus?

Before launching into a full description of radio control equipment which is specially designed for use in helicopter models it is necessary to consider the different ways in which the actual controls used can be arranged.

Consider a typical 4 channel radio control transmitter (Figure 13). This will normally have two control sticks, or 'joysticks', each of which can be moved in two directions. Side to side movement of

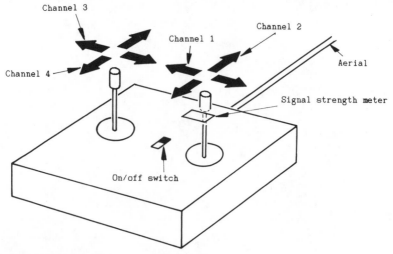

Fig. 13 Typical 4 channel transmitter.

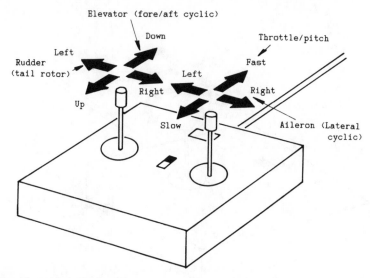

Fig. 14 Mode 1 stick layout.

the stick will operate one control, while up and down movement will operate a second control. There are two basic control layouts, or 'modes', which are used for both conventional models and helicopters. These modes are known as 'Mode 1' and 'Mode 2' (all very logical). In normal use very few people seem able to

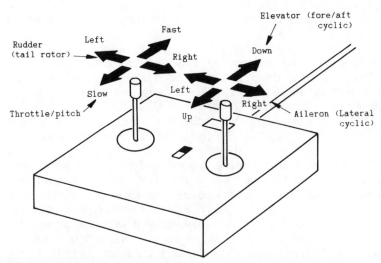

Fig. 15 Mode 2 stick layout.

27

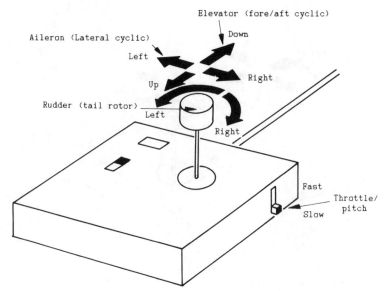

Fig. 16 Mode 3 stick layout.

remember just which one is which so they are more usually referred to as 'throttle right' and 'throttle left'.

In both Mode 1 and Mode 2 transmitters, side to side movements of the joysticks produce exactly the same effects. The right hand stick causes the model to bank to the right or left, while the left hand stick makes it turn, or yaw, to the right or left (Figures 14 and 15).

On a Mode 1 transmitter, forwards and backwards movement of the right hand stick will open or close the throttle (and increase or reduce the pitch on a collective pitch machine) and a similar movement of the left hand stick will cause the model to raise or lower its tail (Figure 14).

Mode 2 transmitters have the fore and aft stick actions interchanged (Figure 15). The terms 'throttle right' or 'throttle left' should now take on some meaning.

For conventional aircraft the two types of transmitter are roughly evenly split throughout the world. For helicopter operation, however, Mode 2 has some advantages in that the right hand stick merely has to be pushed in the direction which you want the helicopter to go. Some people also claim it as an advantage that this system combines the slow acting cyclic pitch controls on one stick and the faster acting throttle and tail rotor controls on the other. Nonetheless, the Mode 1 configuration is used in some parts

28

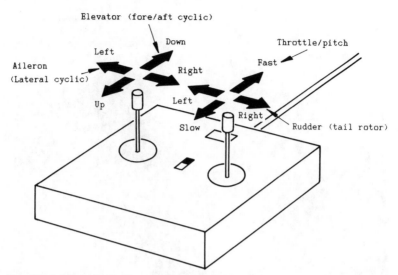

Fig. 17 Left-hand Mode 2.

of the world – notably Japan – and has followers elsewhere (including the writer).

There is one other control layout which has much to offer the helicopter flyer despite the disadvantage of being not generally available from most manufacturers. Known sometimes as Mode 3, this has a single joystick controlling three functions simultaneously. Side to side and fore and aft movement give the same effect as before, but twisting the stick controls the model's yaw axis (Figure 16). The box is normally held in the curve of the left arm and the throttle function is controlled via a lever on the side which is operated by the left thumb.

Other layouts are possible and are sometimes used by individuals or small local groups. One such is what might be called 'left handed Mode 2' (Figure 17). Some people prefer the throttle function reversed so that the stick is pulled towards you to increase power.

Whichever of these arrangements you may fly will usually be determined by the layout most used by the modellers in your local group. This avoids the various problems incurred by 'going it alone' when experienced help is available. Those who are unable to obtain such help must decide for themselves, but if you have no previous radio control flying experience you would be well advised to follow the majority and adopt the Mode 2, or 'throttle left' layout.

Those who have previous experience of fixed wing flying should stay with the arrangement to which they are accustomed. This is

Author David Day flies his *Graupner* 'Helimax' around himself at high speed, like a control-line model. Note that the transmitter tray supports the wrists yet leaves hands free for delicate control movements.

particularly true if you have a considerable amount of flying experience. The writer firmly believes that this is the correct approach despite the fact that many well-known fixed wing fliers have successfully changed from Mode 1 to Mode 2 when taking up helicopter flying.

Neck strap or tray?
Although the vast majority of fixed wing fliers normally hold their transmitter in their hands and control the model with their thumbs, it is normal to use some additional support when flying helicopters. It must be said that there are one or two notable exceptions to this rule, but most people find it difficult to hold the transmitter and exercise the necessary degree of fine control. Usually, it is necessary to hold the stick between the thumb and first finger in order to achieve this.

There are two generally used means of providing this support, a neck strap or a tray. Most of the available transmitters incorporate a loop or eye in the centre of the front panel for the attachment of a neck strap. A suitable strap can be obtained from music shops in the form of a saxophone strap. Most fliers find this quite sufficient for the purpose.

A purpose-made tray to support the transmitter has the disadvantage of being bulkier, despite which many fliers use them and feel that this is the best means of support. It has the advantage of providing both a very stable support for the transmitter and some support for the wrists, which greatly assists in allowing a fine control of the sticks.

Don't be afraid to change your mind
Having adopted a particular control mode or means of supporting the transmitter, don't be afraid to try other arrangements. It may be found that once some experience has been acquired you may become aware of deficiencies or problems in the layout you have adopted. The longer you continue to use an unsatisfactory arrangement, the more difficult it will become to change.

Len and Colin Bliss are father and son and run a specialist helicopter shop. Len learned to fly on Mode 1 (throttle right) and Colin followed suit when he began to fly choppers. As most of their customers flew the Mode 2 arrangement there were obvious benefits to be gained by one of them changing to this layout. Len decided that his flying might benefit from the change and proceeded to try it with the help of Colin and a 'buddy-box' link between two transmitters.

Initially, this seemed to be a success and Len was quite enthusiastic about the results. After about a year he came to the conclusion that the 'throttle left' layout was better for the hovering manoeuvres but that his aerobatic flying had suffered. He further concluded that he was probably too old to change back! Another year's flying, however, convinced him that Mode 2 was not for him and he took the courageous step of returning to Mode 1. Both changes took about six months to effect.

If you are unsure about the set-up that you are using, don't be afraid to try something else. Having done so, don't be afraid to admit that you were wrong if necessary.

Radio control equipment

5

Standard or helicopter radio

We have already briefly described a standard 4 channel (or 4 function) radio control outfit. It has also been explained that the inexperienced flier, whether he be inexperienced in just helicopters or in all types of radio controlled flying, would be well advised to avoid a special helicopter radio at first unless experienced help is available. Readers who fall into this category may find all or part of the ensuing description of helicopter radios rather heavy going at this stage, in which case it might be as well to delay reading this

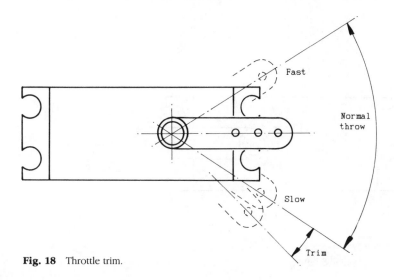

Fig. 18   Throttle trim.

particular chapter and return to it after digesting more immediately important passages. Nonetheless, a description of helicopter radios should be included at this stage in order to give a consistent coverage of the subject.

The primary difference between a helicopter radio and any other type of radio control equipment lies in the provision of a separate channel for control of the collective pitch. This channel is operated by the throttle stick in parallel with the throttle function, but is otherwise entirely separate. By this means, both the throttle and pitch functions may be individually tailored to suit their specific requirements without affecting each other.

A typical helicopter transmitter will, therefore, be found to have the following trim controls, all of which relate to the action of the throttle stick:

(a) A 'throttle trim' which is only effective on the lower end of the throw and controls tick-over, or idle, speed (Figure 18).
(b) Another throttle trim, usually called 'hovering throttle', which is only effective on the centre part of the throw and controls the hovering speed (Figure 19).
(c) Pitch end point adjustments which set the amount of pitch available at each end of the throttle stick's travel (Figure 20).
(d) A pitch trim control which may affect the whole of the pitch range or, in some cases, just the centre portion of the range and will then be called 'hovering pitch' (Figure 21).

These are just the minimum requirements and a specialised system designed for FAI aerobatic type contest flying will also include high

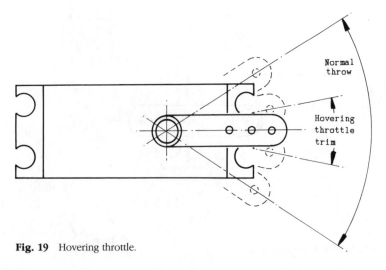

Fig. 19 Hovering throttle.

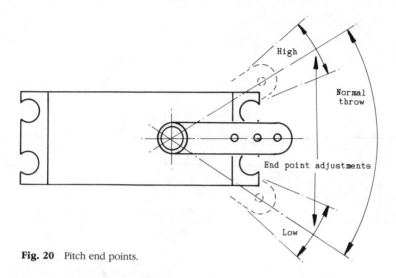

Fig. 20 Pitch end points.

and low pitch trimmers, together with additional pitch end point adjustments associated with the switched throttle options about to be described.

Throttle hold

This control is normally operated by a toggle switch located in an easily accessible position and frequently with an extra long toggle to facilitate operation. Its purpose is to place the throttle servo in a preset position while leaving the pitch servo under full control of the throttle stick. By this means it is possible to practise autorotation landings by setting the motor to idle speed without affecting operation of the pitch channel.

In some specialist systems, operation of the throttle hold switch will bring into operation a separate set of pitch end point adjustments so that these may be set to the optimum values for autorotation. This may be seen as something of a mixed blessing since, in the event of a genuine engine failure, you must remember to flick the 'throttle hold' switch in order to set everything up for a safe landing.

Idle up

Here the purpose is to raise the engine speed at the lower end of the throttle stick (Figure 22) and this is normally brought into effect by a toggle switch similar to the 'throttle hold' switch. There are two reasons why this is needed.

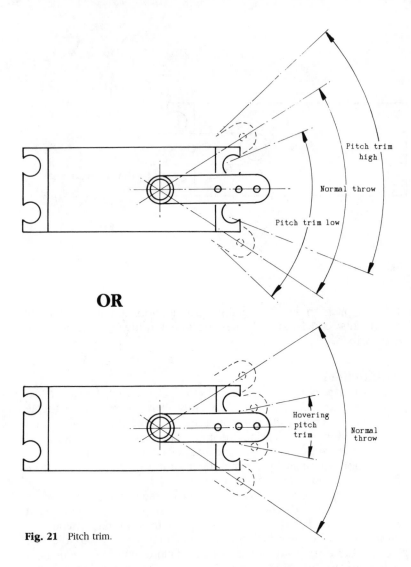

Fig. 21 Pitch trim.

We have already described the problems associated with translating from forward to hovering flight with a fixed pitch machine (Chapter 2). Much the same situation applies to a collective pitch machine which is not fitted with an autorotation clutch (a device which allows the main rotor to 'freewheel' at a higher speed than the drive system). By setting the 'throttle hold' to keep the rotor RPM at around hovering speed while reducing the pitch to zero, or even slightly negative, a rapid descent can be

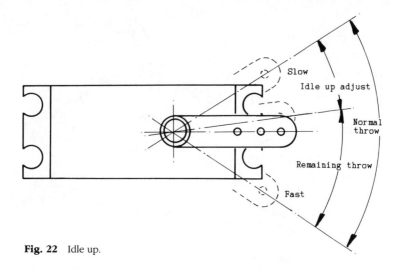

Fig. 22 Idle up.

made without the rotor speed having to be reduced to a point where control is impaired.

When we wish to perform aerobatics, there are numerous instances where it is necessary to be able to apply negative pitch to the rotors without closing the throttle, the inverted part of rolls and the top of loops being obvious examples.

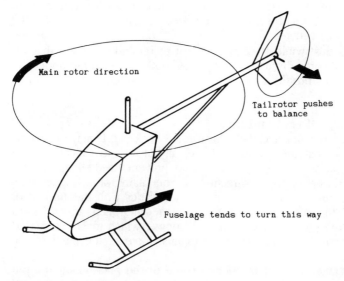

Fig. 23 Tail rotor torque compensation.

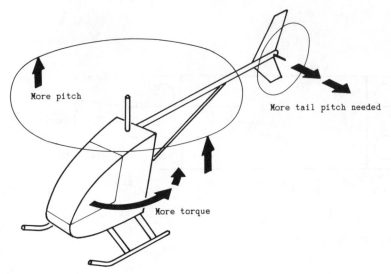

More pitch

More tail pitch needed

More torque

Fig. 24 ATS.

The requirements of the two examples above can be seen to be somewhat different and here again it will be found that the specialist aerobatic system will incorporate two idle up systems which will each have its own pitch end point adjustments to allow exact tailoring for each type of flying. Here it would be normal to use 'idle up 1' for the hovering manoeuvres and 'idle up 2' for the aerobatic manoeuvres.

Perhaps this would be a good point to remind ourselves that, so far, we have only discussed the control options which fall under the control of the throttle stick!

Collective/tail rotor mixing

No, we are not finished with the throttle stick yet! It may be readily understood that the purpose of the tail rotor is to cancel out the torque reaction of the main rotor and prevent the helicopter from rotating in the opposite direction to the main rotor (Figure 23). However, this torque is not constant and varies with the amount of pitch on the main rotor. If we increase the pitch and wish to maintain the same RPM we must add power which means increased torque – which, in turn, means we must increase the pitch of the tail rotor.

This is taken care of by mixing some of the pitch channel input (from the throttle stick!) into the tail rotor (or rudder) channel

The GMP *Competitor* is a fully aerobatic machine for .50–.60 cu.in. engines and can be fitted with a *Jet Ranger* fuselage if desired. This photo clearly shows the swashplate and flybar linkages and, just ahead of the rotor shaft, the cone for use with an electric starter.

(Figure 24). In practice, different requirements exist depending on whether the helicopter is climbing or descending so our helicopter transmitter will have two knobs to adjust the 'up' and 'down' mixing ratios. Also included will be a selector switch to cater for left or right handed rotation of the main rotor together with the ability to switch the mixing off completely.

Here again the more expensive systems will incorporate an additional set of controls to set a different mixing ratio when using the 'idle up 2' facility. This is due to there being differing requirements when the machine is in fast forward flight – as we shall see later.

To sum up, so far, our throttle stick is wholly or partly responsible for the control of three servos – throttle, pitch and tail rotor.

Some sets do cater for fixed pitch machines by the provision of a type of throttle/tail rotor mixing which applies tail correction for a short period of time only and then decays back to the original setting. This is because adding power in these machines necessarily results in an increase in RPM which produces extra thrust from the tail and gives an automatic compensation. Thus, a change of tail rotor pitch is only required to cover the period taken for the system to accelerate. Both the pitch change and the decay time are normally made adjustable so that the system can be set up to suit the individual model.

While this may be seen as a useful feature, there would seem to be little point in purchasing such a set of equipment solely for the flying of a fixed pitch model helicopter. Its cost would only be justified if it was also to be used for the flying of collective pitch models.

Cyclic/collective pitch mixing (CCPM)
All model helicopters incorporate a device known as a swashplate. This enables the various cyclic control inputs to be transmitted from the stationary fuselage to the revolving rotor (Figure 25). In many designs the collective pitch variation is effected by moving the swashplate up and down (Figure 26). Some of the more expensive radio systems allow the linkages of this type of control to be considerably simplified by mixing the collective pitch input into three servos. By moving differentially or collectively, these servos produce all of the necessary swashplate movements for both cyclic and collective pitch inputs (Figure 27).

It should be noted, however, that this system will not work with all moving swashplate designs. Some of these require only the lateral cyclic and collective inputs to be mixed, with the fore/aft

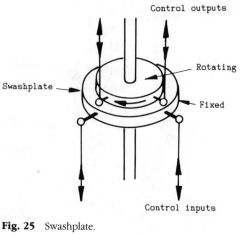

Control outputs

Rotating

Swashplate

Fixed

Control inputs

Fig. 25 Swashplate.

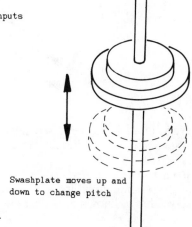

Swashplate moves up and down to change pitch

Fig. 26 Moving swashplate.

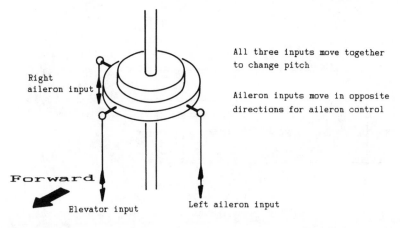

All three inputs move together to change pitch

Aileron inputs move in opposite directions for aileron control

Right aileron input

Forward

Elevator input

Left aileron input

Fig. 27 CCPM.

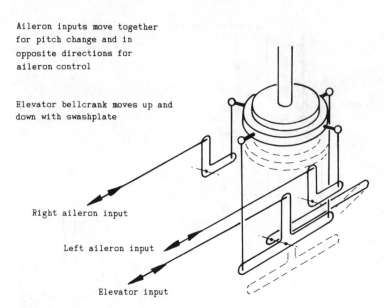

Aileron inputs move together
for pitch change and in
opposite directions for
aileron control

Elevator bellcrank moves up and
down with swashplate

Right aileron input

Left aileron input

Elevator input

Fig. 28 Heim system.

cyclic input being kept separate. One example of this is the Heim
system already mentioned (Figure 28).

Dual rates

Most systems now include a switchable means of reducing the
servo throw, known as a dual rate system. This gives full throw with

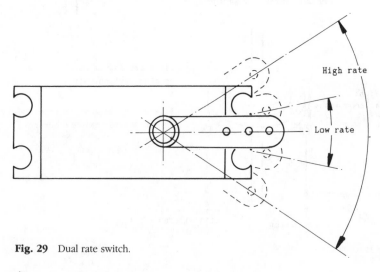

High rate

Low rate

Fig. 29 Dual rate switch.

the switch in one position (though this throw too may be adjustable) and an adjustable reduced throw with the switch in its other position (Figure 29).

This feature is regarded with mixed feelings by many people since a situation can arise where having the switch in the wrong position can be dangerous and lead to a crash. However, it has many advantages and the individual modeller must decide for himself whether the risk is justified. If in doubt simply set both positions of the switch to give maximum throw – then there is no 'wrong' position.

Normally this feature will be found only on lateral and fore/aft cyclic (aileron and elevator) controls and sometimes on tail rotor (rudder).

One peculiarity of many dual rate switches is that the normal, or high, rate is obtained with the switch in the down, or low, position; with the up, or high, position giving the low rate!

Exponential rates

Usually found only on the more expensive equipment, this is a system which gives a reduced throw around the centre of the stick movement with an increasing throw as the stick is moved further and further (Figure 30). The response is, therefore, non-linear but not really exponential in the true sense. A truly exponential system (Figure 31) would require very complex circuitry and it is doubtful whether many people could tell the difference.

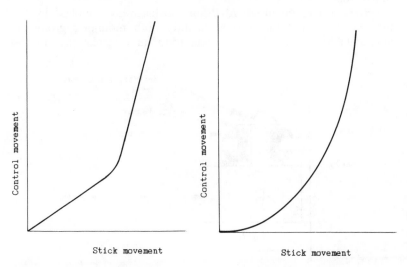

Fig. 30 Exponential (dogleg) rate.   **Fig. 31** True exponential rate.

Indeed, there is some doubt whether the 'dogleg' response of Figure 30 is really detectable, since many contend that the human brain prefers a linear control anyway. There is no disputing that fliers who have tried the so-called exponential rates are either very much for or very much against them. The writer freely admits that he cannot tell the difference!

Invert switch

Yes, helicopters can fly inverted, although the way in which this is done sounds a little like cheating! When the invert switch is operated, the elevator, collective pitch and tail rotor controls are simultaneously reversed. The collective pitch channel is also offset to an adjustable degree to allow for the fact that more negative pitch is now required.

The actual use of this feature will be covered in a later chapter.

Installation

Installing the radio equipment in any given model is something which requires great care if the best performance is to be achieved. Helicopters are a special case due to there usually being a higher level of vibration present than in a conventional model. This is partly due to there being less of the model itself to absorb vibration and partly due to the radio equipment usually being mounted in much closer proximity to the motor.

Servos should be mounted using the hardware supplied by the manufacturers and this should include both mounting grommets and suitable eyelets. These eyelets form an essential part of the

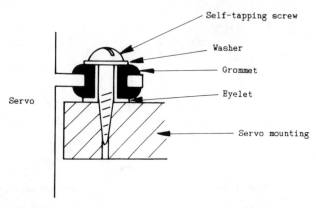

Fig. 32 Correct use of servo grommets.

44

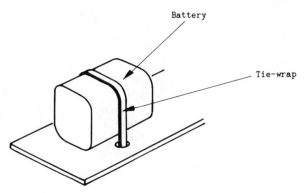

Fig. 33 Method of securing battery pack using nylon tie-wrap.

mounting system and should be so designed that the fixing bolts or screws can be tightened down onto the grommets without actually compressing them. The result of this is to allow the servos to rock on their mountings to absorb vibration without allowing any lateral movement which would interfere with the control action (Figure 32). This particular point cannot be stressed too highly: the servo must be able to move to some extent or its life will be short.

Battery packs must be securely mounted to avoid any possibility of them breaking free in a hard landing. One good way to ensure this is to use a nylon tie-wrap to secure the pack to its mounting platform (Figure 33).

Receivers should be wrapped in foam rubber or plastic and placed so that some movement is possible. One good system here is to use rubber bands to secure the foam-wrapped receiver. If the receiver is in close proximity to the fuel tank, it is a good idea to enclose it in a plastic bag to ensure that any fuel leakage does not penetrate the receiver.

Aerials are a problem on helicopters. This is particularly true of pod and boom types where it is common to see aerials left to hang free and frequently being trodden on. A simple way of avoiding this is to use the outer section of a nylon in nylon control linkage, commonly known as a 'snake', together with two ball joint connectors to form an aerial 'wand' which can be attached to the undercarriage by two self-tapping screws (Figure 34). With a little experimentation it is possible to find a combination which gives a tight fit between the tube and connectors.

A good general rule of all radio installations is that the aerial must be kept as far away as possible from all other wiring and that the aerial itself should be kept in as straight a line as possible. Modern radio equipment is very forgiving and will probably work

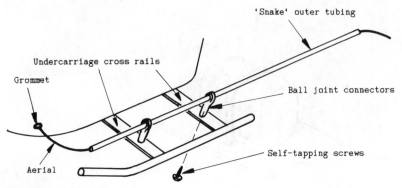

'Snake' outer tubing

Undercarriage cross rails

Grommet

Ball joint connectors

Self-tapping screws

Aerial

Fig. 34 Aerial 'wand'.

quite satisfactorily if you disobey all of these rules. However, it does no harm to load the odds in your favour.

See Appendix 3 for details of available helicopter radios.

New or second-hand

6

Pros and cons

While there can be no disputing the fact that it is possible to pick up some incredible bargains in second-hand helicopter/radio combinations, nonetheless there are many pitfalls to trap the unwary.

One big mistake, which it is difficult for the inexperienced to avoid, is that of purchasing a model which is no longer, or never was, widely available and for which spares are impossible to obtain. If complete and in working order, the model can still be a bargain - - until you crash it!

Unfortunately, there are many helicopter designs around which had a very short production life, simply because they were bad designs. The only way to avoid being saddled with one of these is to avoid anything which you have never heard of, or cannot find advertised in a current copy of any good R/C model magazine. This way you can still make a mistake – but at least the odds are on your side.

Ideally, you should purchase a well-known make which is available from a specialist helicopter shop which is in easy reach of your home. Yes, I appreciate that you may live hundreds of miles from any model shop, but I did say 'ideally'. If you are in this unhappy position, my honest advice would be 'don't buy second-hand' but that too may not be a realistic answer if finance is limited.

Right then, you have a limited amount of money to spend on a second-hand helicopter and must purchase it unseen from a magazine advertisement. Just how do you avoid buying a heap of rubbish?

Anyone who looks after his purchases would normally be expected to keep the instructions and any drawings in good condition and in a safe place. Enquire whether the model being sold is complete with all drawings and instructions. If it is not, then don't buy it. This is not an absolute guarantee of quality, of course, but it is a helpful indication.

If you are purchasing a complete model, engine and radio combination, do try to ensure that all the items are compatible and not just a collection of discarded items from different models. There really is no substitute for being able to see the goods before you buy. Even seeing may not be enough if you are totally inexperienced. If possible insist on a flight demonstration. If the seller cannot fly then everything should obviously be brand new – if it is not, avoid it like the plague – its either third-hand or has seen a lot of punishment.

If you have the finance to allow you to pick and choose then I would suggest that you buy from a specialist helicopter shop as already mentioned. Obviously they will be reluctant to deal in any second-hand items that they themselves are not absolutely sure of. They will be happy to give you a demonstration and will usually be prepared to help you over the initial learning stages. It will cost you a little more perhaps, but it will probably be cheaper in the long run.

What you should not expect is to be able to buy a model of indeterminate condition from a magazine advert and then go along to a specialist shop and get them to help you with it. Don't be surprised if they are unhelpful – if the situation were reversed so would you be!

To sum up, the preferred approach should be as follows, the first listed being the most expensive, the last the least advised:

(1) Buy a well-known design new from a specialist shop.
(2) Buy a well-known design second-hand from a specialist shop.
(3) Buy a well-known design, which is available from a nearby specialist shop, from a magazine advert after seeing it fly and ensuring that it is in good condition and complete with all instructions, drawing, etc.
(4) As item 2 above but without flight demonstration.
(5) As item 3 but unseen.
(6) Buy a well-known design when you have no access to a specialist shop.
(7) Buy a little-known design.
(8) Buy anything.

A few don'ts
Assuming that you are able to inspect before you buy – and

logically you would be unwise to buy anything which you have not seen – then don't accept any of the following:

(1) A helicopter which shows obvious signs of having been bent and then straightened. Alignment is very critical for trouble-free running.
(2) Repaired or very tatty main rotor blades. They are usually an indication of bent shafts and worn gears.
(3) Motors which are caked with castor oil. This is usually an indication of overheating.
(4) Grubby or oily radio equipment. If it was too much trouble to clean the radio, it does not speak well for the model's maintenance.
(5) Radio servos which have cracked or broken lugs. Usually a sign of poor installation.
(6) Servos which have fixing screws which are tightened down hard against the grommets. Servos must be able to move slightly to absorb vibration.
(7) One final rule – if in doubt – don't.

Selling

Before leaving the subject of second-hand equipment, perhaps a word to those who may be selling will be in order. If you want to realise the maximum price for anything you may wish to sell it should be fairly obvious that you should have looked after it and kept it in good order. It is a good selling point if you have kept all of the original boxes, instructions, plans, etc.

If you have time on your side, advertise the equipment in the 'for sale' section of the classified adverts of a model magazine. The higher the circulation of the magazine the better. Such advertisements will, of course, cost you money but it is usually well spent. A specialist shop is not a good idea, here perhaps the following true story will explain why:

A lady entered a specialist helicopter shop accompanied by an older woman. Between them they were carrying a medium sized helicopter complete with motor and radio equipment plus a flight box with electric starter and battery. The lady explained that she and her husband were emigrating to Portugal in a couple of days and she had been given the task of selling the model which was less than two months old and unflown. Her husband had informed her that the complete set-up had cost around £1,000 and she was to obtain as much as possible for it.

The shop proprietor, from whom the equipment must have been purchased, he being the sole importer, stated categorically that it could not possibly have cost more than half of that amount. He then proceeded to explain that the best way to sell it would be via a magazine advert when she might expect to get around half of its value, say £250. However, if she wished the shop to purchase it then they would have to offer the new buyer a guarantee and make a profit so they could not offer her more than about £150 for the lot. The writer looked on in some amazement since a quick mental calculation showed that the as-new cost would indeed be a minimum of around £950.

One is tempted to wonder what price might have been offered had the husband been present or if the departure had not been quite so imminent. To the lady's credit she refused the offer and took the model away with her.

Balancing

7

Static and dynamic

Balancing of any revolving body is a very complex subject which could easily fill a complete book of its own. The method about to be described for the balancing of main rotors has been established as just one of many methods which can be used to give satisfactory results. However, let us try first of all to explain the difference between static balance and dynamic balance.

If we imagine two people of different weights sitting on a see-saw (Figure 35) we can easily see that they must sit at different distances from the pivot in order to balance each other. If A weighs twice as much as B then B must sit twice as far out in order for the see-saw to balance. This is called 'static' balance and it can be seen that the system is only balanced in one position.

When this system is revolved at a high speed it will not be in balance for much of the time and a lot of vibration will result

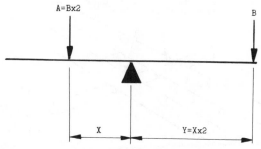

Fig. 35 See-saw.

Fig. 36 Revolving see-saw.

(Figure 36). This is because the system is 'dynamically' unbalanced. What this means, in other words, is that a system which is in balance when it it not moving (i.e. static) is not necessarily in balance when it is moving.

In order to avoid a lot of theory – most of which the writer does not understand either – let's just take it as a fact that in order for our pair of rotor blades to be dynamically balanced we must satisfy just two conditions:

(a) They must both have exactly the same weight.
(b) The centre of gravity (C of G) must be in exactly the same place on each blade.

Note that we are not talking about balancing the rotor head at this stage – we'll cover that a little later – just the blades.

There are two ways to go about achieving this situation: either match the weights and then adjust the C of G position or adjust the C of G positions first and then match the weight by ballasting on the C of G.

Which method you use depends on the equipment available and the initial state of the blades. If you possess an accurate set of scales or a chemical balance, it is probably best to match the weights first. However, if the blades have widely different weights to begin with it is better to match the C of Gs first. Important: Note

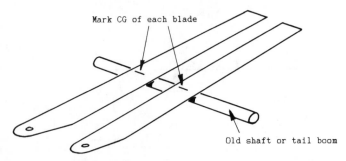

Fig. 37 Blade C of G location.

52

that until the C of Gs have been matched you cannot match the blade weights by bolting them together, or to the head, and balancing them as a pair.

Before we go any further, let us talk about ways of checking, and matching, the blades' centres of gravity. For all practical purposes we can assume that all commercially made blades are fairly consistent and there should not be any variation in the chordwise (that means across the width) position of the C of G. Check if you like, but I doubt whether it is possible to locate it accurately enough to tell the difference without special equipment. This is a long-winded way of saying that we will only bother with the spanwise (along its length) location of the centre of gravity of each blade.

Having checked that both blades are exactly the same length from the fixing hole to the tip, balance them across some suitable object. I use an old Kalt shaft set on the worktable (Figure 37), since the slot for the pitch pushrod stops it from rolling. Many people use the tailboom of the model. Carefully mark the C of G of each blade so that you can compare them. Assuming that there is a fairly small difference this can be corrected by wrapping strips of covering material or ordinary sticky tape around the end of one blade. If a lot of tape is required, then add tape to both blades – at opposite ends, of course – until the C of Gs coincide. Having done that you can now bolt the blades together by their fixing holes and balance them as a unit (Figure 38). Don't bolt them to the rotor head to achieve this unless you have already checked that the head itself is balanced and symmetrical. Tape should be added to the lighter blade at its C of G until they balance.

The problem with the above method is that you can end up with a lot of tape scattered about all over the blades. It is much more efficient, if you have the equipment, to match them for weight first by temporarily adding tape to one blade and then moving it around to match the C of Gs. If there is insufficient for the job then add tape to both blades as before. All this can be done either before or

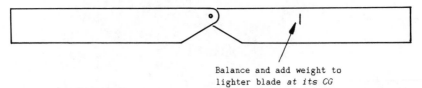

Bolt blades together by fixing holes

Balance and add weight to lighter blade *at its CG*

Fig. 38 Blade balancing as a unit.

53

The KKK Robinson R22HP, available for 10cc glow motors or with a 22cc petrol engine, is unusual in that it uses a flybarless rotor, currently the only such machine in production.

after covering the blades. It is neater to do it before covering and adding equal areas of covering material to each blade will not normally upset your careful balancing, but it pays to check.

Exactly the same procedure can be applied to balancing the tail rotor blades. Normally, you do not need to be quite so fussy with the tail blades though, unless you have a vibration problem. If your particular model is supplied with plastic tail blades do not assume that this means that they are already balanced. If one blade is heavier, the simplest solution is to sand it all over with medium wet and dry paper, used wet, until the weights match.

Blade covering

There are many possible ways of finishing your rotor blades. You could, for instance, use a dope, tissue, sanding sealer type finish or just about any other method normally used to finish model aircraft right up to a glass cloth and resin type finish. Many of these, however, would probably make it very difficult to balance the blades adequately. Incidentally, assume for the moment that we are talking about wooden blades; we'll discuss other materials later.

Generally blades are supplied in one of two forms – finished or unfinished. The finished type include Kalt standard blades which are coated with some form of finishing resin, or the ready painted blades supplied with the Hirobo 'Shuttle'. Unfinished blades are usually intended to be covered with some form of adhesive material such as Fablon. One problem with this material is that it usually has a matt surface which picks up dirt very easily. A very similar, but superior, material is Fas-Cal which appears to originate in both Germany and the USA and has a glossy finish. A range of colours caters for any taste but the writer's preference is for glossy white which makes the rotor disc very visible in sunlight and is a great aid to orientation.

Assuming that you are going to use this type of covering, start off by giving the bare blades a couple of coats of clear dope, sanding after each one. This toughens the surface and gives a good base for painting the roots and tips of the blades in the colour of your choice. Humbrol enamel works well here, and it is fuelproof, comes in umpteen colours and can be matt, glossy, or even semi-matt (now there's a contradiction in terms!). Paint the tips different colours to aid in tracking. Now balance the blades as described above.

Cut two pieces of covering material long enough to cover your blades from $\frac{1}{2}$-$\frac{3}{4}$ inch from the tip to as close as possible to any root reinforcement. The width should be twice the blade chord plus $\frac{1}{4}$ inch (Figure 39). Check that the blade to be covered is free of dust and lay the covering material in position on the top surface

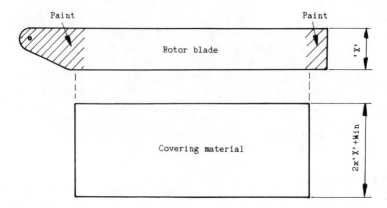

Fig. 39 Blade covering.

with ¼ inch overlap over the trailing edge. It saves time to remove the backing material from the covering before doing this!

After smoothing down into position, wrap the projecting ¼ inch around the trailing edge and smooth that down too. Finally, wrap the remaining material around the leading edge and smooth that down. A section through the finished blade will look like Figure 40. Note that the joint in the covering is a trailing joint so that the airflow will not tend to lift it, and on the bottom of the blade where it is less noticeable.

One possible disadvantage of this system is that it does move the centre of gravity of the blade towards the trailing edge which is generally regarded as undesirable. This can be countered by using covering material which is three blade chords wide and attaching as shown in Figure 41. However, this is a much more tricky operation and not recommended for a first attempt. It is unlikely that the lateral position of the blades' centre of gravity will be a matter of importance to the beginner anyway – he has much more pressing problems to consider.

An alternative method

Another blade covering material which is gaining in popularity is heat shrink tubing. This is available in various colours and

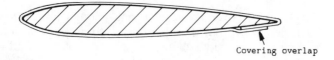

Covering overlap

Fig. 40 Section through blade with adhesive covering.

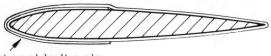

Overlap right round leading edge

Fig. 41 Alternative section through blade.

thicknesses. Be warned, however, that the various colours seem to have different shrinking characteristics, so do some experimenting before actually covering a blade to check on this.

One problem, however, with this material lies in ensuring that exactly the same amount of material is applied to each blade since it is difficult to control the lengthwise shrinkage. The best method would appear to be to cut two identical lengths which are somewhat longer than the blades to be covered and to clamp one end in a vice and then hang on to the other end with your free hand while shrinking with a heat gun (Figure 42). After shrinking the ends can be trimmed and sealed with cyanoacrylate glue. Beware of trying to tidy the ends with more heat, however, since this can produce very uneven shrinking and wrinkling.

From observation it would appear to be difficult to achieve a really neat and tidy job using this material, but it is claimed to have definite advantages such as giving a cleaner aerodynamic profile (less drag) and possible greater structural integrity. It is also lighter than the self-adhesive coverings. Some sources do claim that this material has disadvantages when used on very high revving helicopters in that the covering can be sucked away from the blade by the airflow, causing instability and vibration.

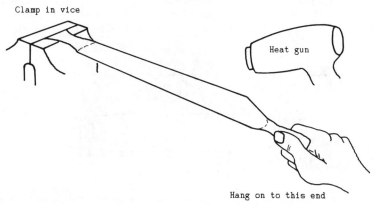

Clamp in vice

Heat gun

Hang on to this end

Fig. 42 Method of shrinking heat shrink covering.

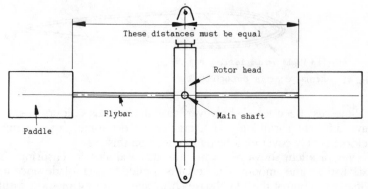

These distances must be equal

Rotor head

Flybar

Main shaft

Paddle

Fig. 43 Checking paddle spacing.

Head balancing

Before you can balance your rotor head and blades as a complete unit the head itself should be balanced and checked for symmetry. First ensure that the flybar paddles are equidistant from the shaft centreline (Figure 43). Then make certain that the blade fixing bolts are exactly the same distance from the shaft centre (Figure 44). Now check the balance of the flybar assembly. This can normally be done by supporting the head without any linkages attached so that the flybar is completely free to rotate about its teeter bearings (Figure 45). The whole assembly is normally free enough to detect a very small imbalance in the flybar and paddles.

Having set the paddles as per Figure 43 they should, in theory, be balanced but this is rarely the case. If there is a very small imbalance this can be put right by adding tape to one paddle. Any large discrepancy should be investigated and the cause found. Usually you will find that one paddle is heavier than the other. Check that both paddles are of identical size and correct if

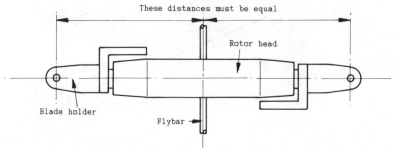

These distances must be equal

Rotor head

Blade holder

Flybar

Fig. 44 Checking blade holder spacing.

58

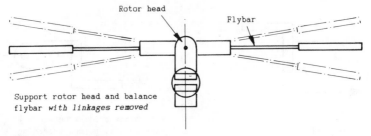

Rotor head

Flybar

Support rotor head and balance
flybar *with linkages removed*

Fig. 45 Flybar balance.

necessary. Where there is no visible difference in size, the heavier
paddle should be sanded all over with medium wet and dry paper,
used wet, until they balance.

Next use the flybar as a pivot to check the balance of the head
along the blade axis (Figure 46). Here again, leave the linkages off
to avoid stiffness. It is unusual to find an out of balance condition
here but, if there is, carefully recheck that both blade holders are
exactly the same distance from the main shaft centreline. If there is
any axial play in the blade holder bearings, the holders should be
pulled outwards to take this up before balancing (Figure 47).

Now you can fit the blades to the head and check the complete
assembly for final balance. If you have a problem here, then the
only real solution is to go back over the whole routine step by step
until you find where the trouble lies.

Vibration

However carefully you may go about the whole balancing
procedure you may still have a vibration problem when the
machine is run. This can originate from many places. Some
machines employ a cone start device which is operated by an
extension shaft attached to the shaft of the motor and extending

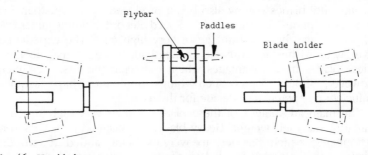

Flybar

Paddles

Blade holder

Fig. 46 Head balance.

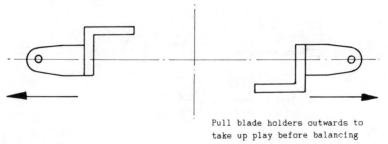

Pull blade holders outwards to
take up play before balancing

Fig. 47 Removing play from holders.

through the clutch. This needs great care in setting up and many people advise the use of an engineer's dial gauge to set it up to give minimum 'run-out'.

The following simple rules can give some guide as to the origin of any vibration:

(a) If the undercarriage shakes, the imbalance is in the motor/ clutch assembly. For some reason you will invariably find that only one skid of the undercarriage will vibrate and this is the one on the side of the advancing main rotor blade (left hand side on clockwise main rotors).

(b) An out of balance main rotor will cause the tail to shake from side to side. Don't confuse this with a low speed oscillation which can be caused by a too-sensitive gyro.

(c) If the tail vibrates up and down, this is caused by an out of balance tail rotor.

Alternative blade materials
Blades are also available from several sources made of glass reinforced plastic (GRP). Both Kalt and Heim produce blades in this material to suit their various models. A range of very high quality GRP blades is now also being produced by the Austrian Sitar brothers, famous for their World Speed Record holding gliders. All of these have the disadvantage of very high cost. The experienced flyer who wishes to compete in aerobatic contests may feel that these blades have advantages which outweigh the cost. Beginners, however, should forget such things until they have acquired sufficient competence to decide for themselves.

The main advantages of these blades is their very high structural integrity and their weight. Heavy blades are claimed to have several advantages, which has led to weights being added to wooden blades, a move which has led to some controversy and caused the

60

International body governing all matters pertaining to all types of model aircraft, the FAI, to ban metal weights in blades.

Weighted blades

Possibly one of the most contentious issues in model helicopter flying is that concerning the matter of weighting blades. The FAI is quite clear in its views on the matter – it should not be permitted. However, when the rules were written they said that metal weights should not be allowed. Little did they realise the devious nature of the average contest flyer who promptly went about finding a non-metallic substance with which to weight his blades! So, accepting that weighted blades are here to stay – for the moment anyway – just why do blades need to be weighted and how do you go about it?

First of all let's add our usual little note for the complete novice. You do not need weighted blades yet. They will not help you to learn to fly and they will cause much more damage in the event of a crash due to their greater inertia.

The most obvious reason for adding weight to a helicopter rotor blade is to increase its inertia and give more margin for auto-rotation landings. This can make all the difference between a heavy 'arrival' and a gently landing on some machines, while on others, if you had plenty of margin anyway, it can allow you to hover for a while to line up on a given spot. If this were the only reason for adding weight, however, then it would obviously not be too critical just where, or how, the weight was added.

It is when the other reasons for adding weight are considered that things become rather more complicated. There are, for example, very good reasons for moving the centre of gravity of the blade towards the leading edge. This makes the blade much more stable and less prone to flutter and other undesirable effects. Increasing the blade mass also makes the whole helicopter more stable and smoother flying due to the increased flywheel effect. If the maximum benefit from this effect is to be achieved, then it is obviously best to add the weight as near as possible to the blade tip.

One other reason for adding blade weight is that it allows a lower rotor speed to be used without running into undesirable effects such as 'nodding', etc. This is where the tail of the model oscillates up and down at a fairly slow speed. The reasons for this are not wholly understood, but it is generally agreed that the effect can be reduced by increasing the rotor RPM, running with the blade fixing bolts very loose, or increasing the blades' weight.

So far we have only considered what might be called the

Vago Nordigian is a display pilot extraordinaire. He can fly his Heim *Star Ranger* as though on a fishline off the end of his transmitter aerial. Here Vago is circling himself, and delayed shutter speed on the camera helps to emphasise value of white (Sitar moulded) blades for visibility.

conventional helicopter, by which we mean one having a flybar with stabiliser paddles. When we consider the use of flybarless heads it is virtually essential to use weighted blades. However, this is outside the realm of our current discussion and will be returned to later.

Having decided that our ballast should be added as far forward as possible and as close to the tip as possible, you will probably be wondering if there are any disadvantages. Well, obviously if you add too much weight you will have a rock solid flywheel on top of your model which will make it almost impossible to control. Until recently, it was generally agreed that six ounces was about the optimum weight for each blade. It now seems to be accepted that the correct figure may be as high as 8 ounces. A typical blade as supplied for most machines currently available would weigh around $3\frac{1}{2}$-$4\frac{1}{2}$ ounces, which means that you will need to add at least $1\frac{1}{2}$-$2\frac{1}{2}$ ounces of weight to each blade.

Obviously, if you are going to add this amount of mass to your blades you are moving into a potentially very dangerous area – which is where we started – and you must give serious thought to whether you want to go ahead and take the risk or forget the whole thing. If you do go ahead you must satisfy yourself that the method of attaching the weight is quite safe, which we will come to in a moment.

Types of weight

First of all, of course, you must decide just what you are going to use to increase the mass of your blades. If you are only using the model for sport flying, or learning to do autorotations, you could use metal. However, in this situation you may be better advised to consider whether you really need weighted blades anyway. It is those who are going to fly in FAI type contests who will probably consider it essential to use some form of heavy blades and they must use some other form of weight. By now you will be asking just how anyone can tell what substance you are using anyway and the answer is quite simple – with a metal detector.

However, it did not take long for someone to discover that finely powdered non-ferrous metals do not show up on metal detectors! The favourite material for this is bronze or a similar fairly heavy metal and the trick is to mix it with epoxy or polyester resin to form a paste. This is then added to suitable holes (Figure 48) in the tip of the blade. *Do be warned that some non-ferrous metals in powder form are highly toxic.* (Beryllium-copper is LETHAL!). Hopefully the dangerous ones will be very difficult to obtain but do check.

A far easier alternative is to use a substance known as 'fisherman's weight' which is available from fishing shops (there's a coincidence) and is intended as a substitute for lead fishing weights. Unfortunately it is only about one quarter as dense as lead which explains why it is not too popular with non-ecologically minded fishermen.

Referring back to Figure 48, do please note that the holes are countersunk so as to provide a solid key to help to keep the weight in position. This area should also be further reinforced by one of the various forms of blade covering described earlier. Most blades are of a composite balsa/hardwood construction and it should be obvious that the weight should only be added to the hardwood section of the blade.

Obviously, if you are going to add weight to your blades, this must be done before balancing. It should be borne in mind that the whole process of balancing will now be much more critical and more difficult. Both the amount and the positioning of the added weight must be identical on each blade in order to meet the conditions for correct dynamic balancing.

Flybarless rotor heads

At one time it was considered that the so-called flybarless head was the way to go for increased manoeuvrability. This was because this type of head does give a much quicker control response due to control inputs being made directly into the blade instead of going through the stabiliser bar system first. In practice it was found that the response was too fast and the model was virtually unflyable. The cure for this was to use heavier blades to slow down the response and smooth things out. As a result of this the overall

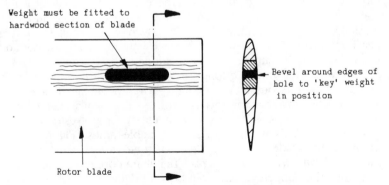

Fig. 48 Holes for blade weighting.

64

handling characteristics became very much a compromise influenced by control geometry, blade weight and several other factors.

At the time of writing (early 1986) there are now very few flybarless helicopter models available. Research and development on the subject is, however, continuing. This is particularly aimed at producing a practical multi-bladed system for scale models.

John Griffiths of *Slough R/C Models* is one experimenter who has dabbled at length in multi-bladed systems and relates the tale of a scale five bladed head which showed promising results. After steadily increasing the weight of the blades a point was reached where the model was beautifully stable in the hover. Unfortunately, attempts to control the beast now merely moved the fuselage about under the rock solid rotor disc.

Eventually, the whole model tilted over and flew into the ground with the fuselage still vainly trying to influence it!

8 Gyrostabilisers

What is it?

A gyrostabiliser consists of a small, rapidly spinning motor-driven flywheel which is able to sense movement of a model about any chosen axis and apply a cancelling movement to the appropriate servo. This description is deliberately chosen to be non-specific since a gyrostabiliser can be used on any axis of any type of model. For reasons which need not concern us here they have become almost solely used on the tail rotor servo of model helicopters to assist in controlling the tail. For this reason they are more generally known as tail rotor gyros or just gyros.

Note that the word used was to 'assist' in controlling the tail. There are still many people who think (perhaps a better word would be 'hope') that a gyro can do all the work of controlling the tail and thus leave the pilot free to concentrate on other things. A moment's thought will show that this ideal state cannot possibly exist, since a gyro cannot react to something until after that something has already happened; even the best of gyros will always be a little too late to prevent any unwanted movement.

What a gyro does do, however, is to damp out unwanted movements and allow the pilot more time to react. It is worth pointing out here that virtually all of the currently best model helicopter pilots learned to fly them before the existence of a practical gyrostabiliser. They did it 'the hard way' and so can anyone else with sufficient determination. The gyro has made it much easier to learn to fly, but once you overcome the basic hurdle they merely serve to smooth out things and make your flying tidier.

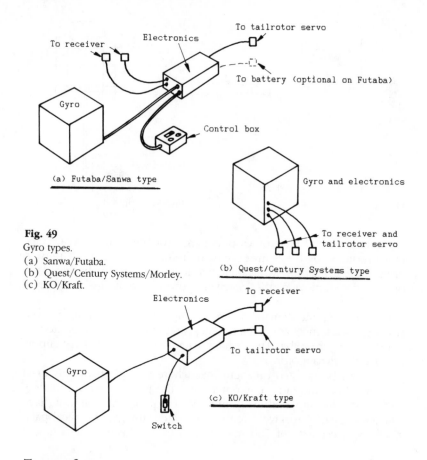

Fig. 49
Gyro types.
(a) Sanwa/Futaba.
(b) Quest/Century Systems/Morley.
(c) KO/Kraft.

Types of gyro

It is amazing how the model world can come up with numerous variations on the same basic device. A basic gyrostabiliser consists of the flywheel and its motor plus an electronics package. This is inserted between the receiver and the tail rotor servo. In many cases there will be a second lead to be plugged into the receiver which will enable the gain, or sensitivity, of the gyro electronics to be varied from the transmitter. Here we come to the first of many possible variations in that this alteration of gain may be continuously variable or switched between two different values. These two values can usually be varied by controls mounted on the gyro itself or, in some cases, also changed at the transmitter.

The plot thickens when we consider the mechanical layout of the whole device. Figure 49 shows some of the possible variations. Most units of Japanese origin consist of three packages comprising

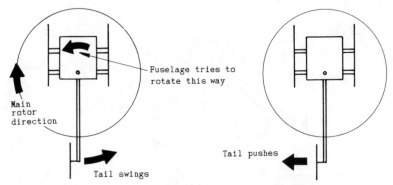

Fig. 50 Torque reaction. **Fig. 51** Tail pitch.

separate gyro and electronics plus a control box (Figure 49a). One unit produced by the Sanwa company requires a separate battery to drive the gyro motor, while that manufactured by Futaba gives the option of employing the receiver power supply or a separate battery.

In the U.K. most manufacturers employ a single unitary construction with mechanics, electronics and controls all mounted in one box (Figure 49b). This usually uses the receiver battery supply to drive the gyro motor.

It should be pointed out here that where a single battery is used to power both the radio equipment and the gyro motor, the battery pack normally supplied with the radio equipment will not have sufficient capacity to give a reasonable safety margin. A typical pack will have a capacity of 500 mAH which in a collective pitch model

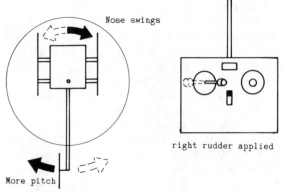

Fig. 52 Tail response to stick.

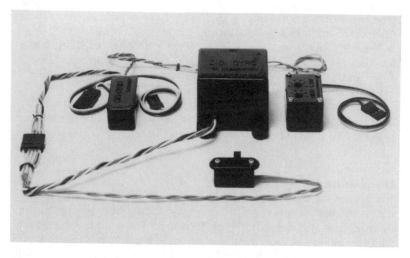

The *Digi Gyro* is an example of a multi-package gyro system with control box, gyro and electronics in separate boxes with a wiring harness.

A one-piece gyro unit is offered by Century Systems and no separate battery is needed. The unit can be bought ready-made or in kit form for home assembly.

employing five servos and a gyro may have a fully charged life of only 20-25 minutes and certainly no more than 1 hour.

Most manufacturers are able to supply a larger capacity battery for this purpose. This will normally have a capacity of 1,000 or 1,200 mAH. Even when this is used it would not be advisable to expect a safe endurance of more than about an hour.

The abbreviation 'mAH' used above stands for milliamphours. A battery of 500 mAH capacity can supply a current of 50 milliamps (mA) for 10 hours (H) or 500 mA for 1 hour, etc.

Installation

Great care should be used in mounting the mechanical portion of the unit. Any vibration which may by transmitted to the motor/flywheel unit will degrade the performance. Some units are supplied with mounting lugs for mounting on rubber grommets like a servo, while others are designed to be mounted using self-adhesive servo tape. The actual orientation of the unit relative to the main shaft of the helicopter is vital to its correct operation and the manufacturer's instructions should be followed implicitly.

If a separate control box is included this should be mounted in a position which allows easy access for adjustment, while the electronics section should be wrapped in foam and installed in a similar manner to the radio receiver. The exact positioning of the various units will depend on your particular model but many helicopter manufacturers now design a gyro mounting platform into their models.

Normally, the instructions included with the gyro will give some guide to assist with initial setting up, but if not place all the various controls at their mid-point. Further adjustment can only be made as a result of the model having been flown.

Adjustment

One essential requirement before attempting to fly a model equipped with a gyro for the first time is to ensure that the gyro is working in the correct sense. This means that if the tail of your model starts to swing towards the left then the gyro must apply a correction which will make the tail move to the right. If not, the gyro will merely aggravate any instability in the model and produce a situation which is beyond the control of any normal pilot.

Obviously, it will be of great help to have the assistance of an experienced flier at this point. However, if you are a total novice and have no help available, proceed as follows:

(a) First of all establish which way your main rotor will be turning. Let's assume for the moment that it rotates in a clockwise direction when viewed from the top. The torque reaction produced by the motor in turning the rotor will make the whole helicopter try to rotate in an anti-clockwise direction (Figure 50) and the tail will tend to swing to the right.

(b) To counteract this, the tail rotor must produce a push to the left and the blades must be set so that normal rotation will produce a thrust in that direction (Figure 51).

(c) When the tail rotor (rudder) stick on the transmitter is moved to the right, the pitch of the tail rotor blades must increase to give more thrust and move the tail to the left – which moves the nose to the right and produces the desired right turn (Figure 52).

(d) With your radio equipment switched on and the gyro running, try moving the tail of the model sharply to the right. The tail rotor servo should move to increase the tail rotor pitch and attempt to move the tail to the left to compensate. If the tail is moved sharply to the left, the tail rotor pitch should automatically be reduced to correct this (Figure 53).

(e) If your model has an anti-clockwise main rotor, all of the above directions will be reversed.

To sum up, first establish that your tail rotor is receiving the correct command from the transmitter and then check that any sudden movement of the tail will produce a cancelling command from the gyro. Note that the amount of the response will be

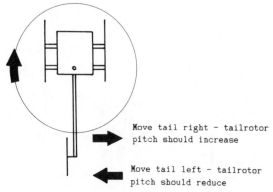

Move tail right – tailrotor
pitch should increase

Move tail left – tailrotor
pitch should reduce

Fig. 53 Tail response to gyro.

controlled by the gain, or sensitivity, set on the gyro electronics. High gain will give a large response and vice versa.

The overall response of the model to a given control input at the transmitter can be varied in several ways. A purely mechanical variation can be effected by changing the relative lengths of the servo arm and the tail rotor pitch control lever. Increasing the length of the servo arm or reducing the length of the pitch lever will give increased response (Figure 54).

Many modern radio control outfits will allow this response to be varied from the transmitter as already described. Here you simply ensure that the mechanical linkage will give more than sufficient control and then adjust the radio transmitter to suit. Note that the transmitter control will only allow you to reduce the response; it cannot give more throw than the mechanical linkage will allow.

Also note that the gyro gain control is similarly limited by the mechanical linkage and this too can only reduce the response.

The novice flier will normally require that the model's response to the transmitter is at a minimum, to avoid any tendency to overcontrol, while the gyro has as much effect as possible to help him during the learning process.

There are two possible pitfalls here of which you must be wary:

(1) The mechanical linkage is set to give a very large control range which is then reduced to manageable proportions by means of the transmitter throw adjustment. This still gives the gyro an oversensitive control and it will be very difficult to set the gyro gain control to give an acceptable response. An overcontrolling gyro will cause the tail to oscillate. In this situation it may be necessary to reduce the gyro gain to such an extent to cure the oscillation that the gyro has little, if any, effect at all.

(2) Conversely, if the model's sensitivity is reduced mechanically to make it easy to fly, the gyro may be left with insufficient control to have any effect.

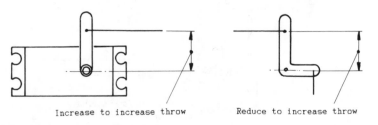

Increase to increase throw   Reduce to increase throw

Fig. 54 Adjustment of mechanical sensitivity.

72

Without its bodywork, the Schluter *SX-81* displays its package of mechanics. Steve Buchanan uses a Webra Speed 61 engine in his, flown in Jersey, Channel Isles.

Both of these situations lead to the conclusion that the gyro is inadequate for its purpose whereas the real problem lies in the adjustment of the model's control linkage. This is where the oft-mentioned experienced help is worth its weight in gold, since the correct set-up can only be established by flying the model and adjusting the linkage and controls to give correct gyro action and then setting the tail up to suit the particular flier.

This one point alone has almost certainly caused many novice fliers to struggle on with an unmanageable model which could easily be completely transformed by correct adjustment.

Stick preferential systems

Some authorities believe that there are advantages to be gained by arranging things in such a manner that the sensitivity of the gyro varies in a way which is dependent on the amount of tail rotor control which is being applied. Usually, this is arranged so that the gyro has a high gain while the rudder stick is at, or close to, the centre position. As the stick approaches its extreme (maximum control) the gyro sensitivity is reduced to near zero.

The reasoning here is that maximum gyro control is only required when the model is desired to remain on a stable heading. If a rapid turn is required, the gyro will tend to oppose this and should, therefore, be given less control.

Not all authorities are in total agreement with this. The Morley gyro, for instance employs a system whereby extreme stick deflection will still allow the gyro to add to the control, but not to reduce it.

It is clear that this particular approach will continue to be developed and that the ultimate system may not yet have been seen.

Incidentally, if your particular radio employs the so-called exponential control on the rudder function and this is used with a normal gyro, the result is exactly the same as a stick preferential gyro. What is more, the effect is fully adjustable.

See Appendix 4 for details of all available gyros.

Training devices 9

Simulators
Some fliers would argue that simulators are of little real use, due mainly to the fact that they do not involve the risk of crashing a model and, therefore, do not give the right degree of mental tension. While it is true that flying a model is very different, simulators do have one very real advantage in that it is not

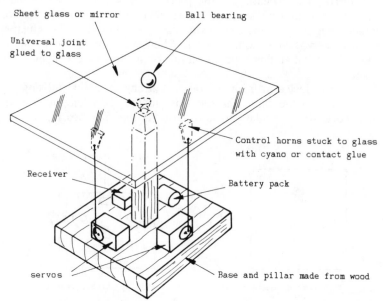

Sheet glass or mirror

Ball bearing

Universal joint glued to glass

Control horns stuck to glass with cyano or contact glue

Receiver

Battery pack

servos

Base and pillar made from wood

Fig. 55 Orientation simulator.

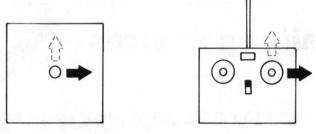

Ball bearing moves in direction indicated by stick movement

Fig. 56 Normal operating position.

necessary actually to purchase – and possibly crash – an expensive model.

At first sight this appears to be the same statement slanted in two different ways. However, the real point is that some intending helicopter pilots simply may not have the necessary co-ordination, or manual dexterity, to succeed. A simulator will show up this fact very quickly and allow such unfortunate individuals to save themselves a considerable financial outlay and a large amount of wasted time.

The simplest form of simulator consists of a sheet of glass, or an old mirror, a ball bearing, some pieces of wood and a set of radio equipment with two servos (Figure 55). Any type of radio will suffice, but as you progress you may well find that the cheaper types of servos limit your control. When you become really adept you will find that this type of simulator makes an excellent servo tester.

Place the device in front of you and arranged so that moving the cyclic stick to the right tilts the glass to the right and pulling the stick back tilts the glass towards you. If the ball bearing is now

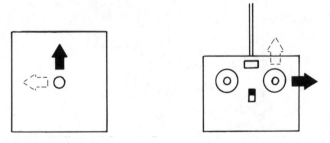

Ball bearing moves in direction indicated by stick movement

Fig. 57 Sideways on position.

76

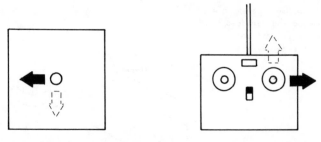

Ball bearing moves in direction indicated by stick movement

Fig. 58 Nose-in position.

placed on the glass it may be made to roll in whichever direction the control sticks are pushed (Figure 56).

With a small amount of practice you will find that it soon becomes possible to steer the ball around the glass without falling off the sides (you could of course put some form of barrier around the sides to prevent this – but that would be cheating). A lot of practice will allow you to place the ball anywhere and follow a complicated shape drawn on the glass. You may feel at this point that you have mastered the device, but no! Try turning the contraption around until you are seeing it sideways on and then start again (Figure 57).

When you have got the better of that one, turn the simulator through another 90° and operate it with the controls completely reversed (Figure 58). This is precisely the situation you will encounter when trying to hover a helicopter with its nose towards you – the so-called nose-in hover.

If you have got this far and are beginning to think there is nothing to it, try holding the ball stationary in the middle of the glass while walking in a circle around the simulator. Should you

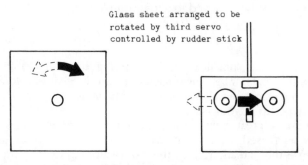

Glass sheet arranged to be rotated by third servo controlled by rudder stick

Fig. 59 3 axis simulator.

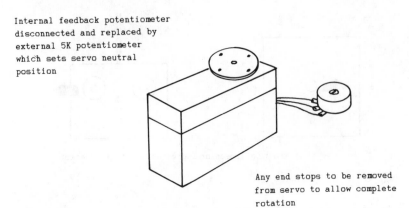

Internal feedback potentiometer disconnected and replaced by external 5K potentiometer which sets servo neutral position

Any end stops to be removed from servo to allow complete rotation

Fig. 60   Servo modifications for 3 axis simulator.

find that that is easy you are obviously a born model helicopter pilot. On the other hand, if you cannot control the ball to a reasonable extent after a couple of evenings' practice I can only suggest that you forget the whole thing.

It is possible to construct a more advanced simulator which uses a modified servo to actually turn the glass around by using the rudder channel. There are many possible ways of arranging the mechanical part of such a device depending on your skills and equipment. One possible 'kitchen table' means of achieving this is shown in Figure 59.

The servo modifications are best left to a knowledgeable friend with some experience of electronics and consist of removing the feedback potentiometer and replacing it with a preset type (Figure 60). This is then adjusted until the servo remains stationary with the control stick at neutral. Any stick offset will cause the servo to move in the appropriate direction at a speed which is controlled by the amount of stick throw. If the servo concerned is fitted with end stops, these must be removed to allow complete rotation.

Floats

Probably the most practical aid to learning to fly is to fit your model with floats. Most manufacturers produce floats for their particular products but it is not very difficult to adapt any of the available types to fit your model.

Floats are a great help during the initial hovering stages since they give increased stability on the ground and in the air. In the former case they greatly reduce the risk of tipping over, particularly if the model is moving sideways along the ground. When airborne their extra drag helps to prevent the model gaining too much speed (and helps to slow it down when required) and also slows down the model's response to any control input, which helps to prevent overcontrolling. Both of these effects are also helpful when attempting your first circuits, for the same reasons.

In the very early learning stage floats also allow you to 'fly' the model along the ground, particularly on grass, and get to know the feel of the controls and the effect of each stick deflection without actually leaving the ground. This skidding around on the ground with the throttle set just below the point of lift-off is sometimes known as the 'zero height hover'.

This is a very useful way of getting used to controlling the tail of the model and learning the relationship between the throttle movement and its effect on the tail.

The Morley string method

Jim Morley is the designer and manufacturer of the *Morley* range of model helicopters. He was, for some years, the author of the 'Hovering About' column in the magazine 'Radio Control Models and Electronics' and during this period devised the training method which requires nothing more than a length of string.

This is, perhaps, a slight oversimplification, since you also need an assistant who, apart from needing a certain amount of courage, should preferably be an experienced model helicopter flier. This experience is not essential, but certainly helpful.

The idea is to attach the length of string to the model's tail in a position which will ensure that it cannot easily become entangled in the tail rotor. Your assistant stands behind the model and holds the other end of the string. When the model is lifted off you should apply a small amount of forward trim, or hold some forward stick,

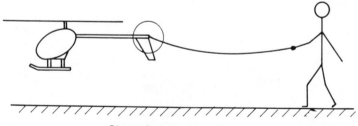

Piece of string securely
attached to rear of model
and held by assistant

Fig. 61 Morley string method.

so that the model is always attempting to move forwards and, therefore, keeps the string tight. The assistant must raise and lower his arm so as to keep the string horizontal and avoid applying any unwanted up or down pull on the model's tail (Figure 61).

This ensures that the model's tail is stabilised by the string and you can concentrate on the business of learning to hover at a constant height and position. Having crossed that hurdle the string tension can be steadily reduced, which will make the pilot do more of the work of controlling the tail and eventually make the string unnecessary.

Training platforms
Various types of devices involving platforms on telescopic mounts or multiple jointed arms have been available from time to time. The writer has no experience of any of these nor has he met anyone who has. Such devices are still available from the Kavan and Schlüter companies.

Hovering 10

R/C set-up for initial attempts

One of the most common types of damage which the novice pilot is likely to inflict on his model is that caused by one of the main rotor blades coming into contact with the tailboom. An examination of any typical model will lead to the conclusion that this is not possible since it will require an unbelievable amount of force to make the blades come anywhere near the boom. Nonetheless, the forces acting upon the model when it is unceremoniously 'dumped' onto the ground to avoid an impending crash are more than adequate to ensure that the seemingly impossible can happen with depressing regularity.

The first sign that you are making real progress in learning to fly is that such mishaps become rarer and, eventually, very unusual, despite the model not having been changed in any way.

Fortunately, assuming that your model is a collective pitch type, it is possible to reduce the chances of this happening in the early stages by setting up the model in a suitable manner. Many manufacturers give details of how the pitch range of their models should be set up. Usually this is aimed at those who can already fly fairly competently and want to perform circuits, or even aerobatics, which means that some amount of negative pitch is required.

For the beginner, however, this negative pitch angle is exactly what is not required and it is recommended that the lowest pitch that the blades can reach should be $+1°$. This ensures that if you suddenly pull the throttle stick hard back and drop the model onto the ground very hard, the blades will still be lifting and not pushing themselves down towards the tailboom. However, don't assume that

The KKK *Hughes 300* is another model from this manufacturer for 10cc glow motors or available fitted with a 22cc petrol engine. Note coloured tips on rotor, a considerable help when checking tracking.

this will provide a complete cure for the problem: it will merely reduce it.

Just how you go about determining the pitch angle of your blades depends to some extent on the make of helicopter which you purchase and also on the depth of your pocket. There are several devices on the market which are designed to measure the pitch angle with varying degrees of accuracy but, like everything else, the good ones are expensive. Some manufacturers supply a wood or plastic template in their kits which will enable you to set the pitch to the recommended range. If one of these is not supplied, it is not too difficult to make your own (Figure 62).

Tracking

In Chapter 7 we talked about blade covering and stated that the blade tips should be of different colours to aid in tracking. When you first run up your model you should carefully observe the blade tips when the model is on the point of lifting off. It is virtually certain that the tips will not be exactly in line with each other. By means of the different colours it should be possible to decide which blade is running high and which low (Figure 63).

The pitch of each blade should be adjusted until both tips are running at exactly the same height, or tracking in exactly the same path. There are several different ways of doing this, depending on the helicopter, and you should refer to the maker's instructions for your particular model.

If you had set the pitch of the blades using a pitch gauge this will, of course, upset your careful adjustments. Here the answer is to be extra careful with the pitch setting of one blade and make all your tracking adjustments to the other blade.

Some types require the 'static' tracking to be set before any

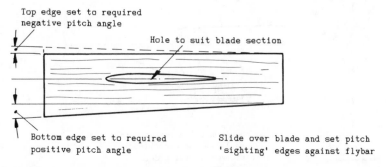

Top edge set to required negative pitch angle

Hole to suit blade section

Bottom edge set to required positive pitch angle

Slide over blade and set pitch 'sighting' edges against flybar

Fig. 62 Home-made pitch gauge.

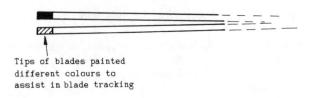

Tips of blades painted
different colours to
assist in blade tracking

Fig. 63 Blade tracking.

running takes place. This is done by setting the model on a flat surface, measuring the height of one blade tip, then rotating the rotor head through half a turn and measuring the height of the other blade. Adjustments may then be made to ensure that both tips are at the same height above the same point without the model being moved (Figure 64).

First attempts

Having set your blade tracking and decided which of the previously discussed training aids you may, or may not, be going to use, you are ready for your first efforts at flying the beast.

It cannot be repeated too often that the main ingredient required by anyone wishing to learn to fly model helicopters is sheer dogged perseverance! There are people in this world who have learned to fly very quickly and with little trouble, but rest assured that they are in a very small minority.

As a general rule it can be said that those who have experience of flying fixed wing models will find helicopters more difficult to fly than those who are starting from scratch. This is a natural result of the fact that the two types are very different and it is necessary to 'unlearn' a great deal before progress can be made.

Assuming that you have to 'go it alone', it is highly recommended

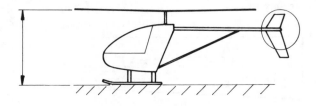

Set model on solid surface and
measure height of each blade in
turn without moving model

Fig. 64 Static tracking.

84

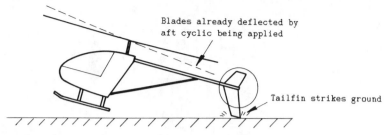

Fig. 65 Tailboom strike.

that the model be fitted with floats for the reasons already given. You will find that in the initial stages it is much easier to control the tail if the model is always kept moving slowly forwards. If you land with forwards movement when skids are fitted there is some danger of them 'digging in' and causing the model to tip over.

Start by increasing power until the model becomes very light on the floats but does not quite leave the ground. You will find that the model can be moved around on the ground in this state and that all the controls are effective. Be careful that you do not apply too much cyclic, however, since this will cause the model to tip over. If the model is in danger of doing so, close the throttle immediately, but smoothly. Try to avoid holding on back cyclic as the throttle is closed since this will increase the possibility of a tailboom strike by the blades.

This is very much a two-edged sword situation, since the only way that the beginner can prevent the model tipping over is to close the throttle, yet any sudden closing of the throttle is to be avoided, for the reasons already given.

Let's have a closer look at the factors involved in the blades striking the tailboom. We have already seen that negative pitch angles should be avoided at this stage. However, even at positive angles a sudden closing of the throttle followed by the model striking the ground can deflect the blades far enough to cause contact. A fairly common situation occurs where the model is moving forwards and the stick is pulled back to stop it, followed by the model hitting the ground in a tail-down attitude. Here we have the blades already being depressed at the rear of the disc by the stick deflection (Figure 65) and the tailboom being suddenly forced upwards by striking the ground. In this situation contact can occur with the throttle set at hovering power and the blades at a high pitch angle and lifting strongly.

The thing to remember here is that the throttle should never be closed suddenly. Even in an emergency situation it should be closed smoothly. Whenever the model touches the ground, always

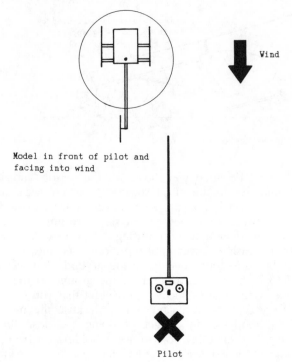

Wind

Model in front of pilot and
facing into wind

Pilot

Fig. 66 Safe base.

try to ensure that it does so in a level, or slightly nose down,
attitude.

Meanwhile, back at the hover

All of your early hovering attempts will be made with the model in
front of you and the tail pointing towards you (Figure 66). When
you have mastered the hover this will become a 'safe base' to
return to when you get into difficulties. There is some danger of
this position becoming the only way that you can fly the model,
with other positions or attitudes becoming increasingly difficult.
While you are at the stage where the model is being slid around in
contact with the ground, perhaps accompanied by the odd short
hop, it is advisable to try manoeuvring the model round in turns,
both left and right, and also positioning the model with its nose
towards you. This will pay dividends later.

After a few sessions of steering the model around on the ground
in a 'zero height hover' you will reach the stage where the power

can be increased in short bursts to lift the model clear of the ground for short periods. One advantage of this approach is that you become accustomed to the throttle setting which will allow the model to settle gently back to the ground rather than falling rapidly.

With increasing confidence you should reach the point where the model can be kept in the air for lengthy periods with it moving slowly forwards and you following it. At this stage, don't be tempted to try to turn the model as this will inevitably lead you into a difficult situation which you will not be able to cope with.

The next hurdle is to stop moving forwards and keep the model stationary over one spot. Having got used to moving forwards, this can produce problems in knowing whether you are moving or not. Some form of marker on the ground is a great help here. This can be a patch of grass or bare earth, a stone, a car mat, etc., but do ensure that it is not large enough to cause problems if the model should touch it.

Stopping the model moving forwards can also be problematical. Obviously, you pull the cyclic stick back to lower the tail and impart a rearwards force to stop the forwards movement. Unfortunately, early efforts are likely to lead to the model charging backwards towards the pilot followed by a large application of forward stick causing an uncontrollable build up of forward speed.

The pendulum concept

Something which may help here is to try visualising the helicopter as being on the lower end of a pendulum with the transmitter controls moving the top of the pendulum. Moving the top of the pendulum to, say, the right will cause the model to move to the

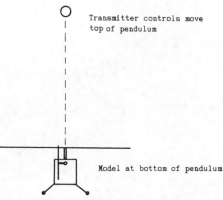

Transmitter controls move top of pendulum

Model at bottom of pendulum

Fig. 67 Pendulum concept.

A situation for the very capable flyer only. The model is dangerously close to the pilot and at this low altitude any slight mistake can be very expensive!

right after a slight delay. In order to stop this movement, the top of the pendulum must now be moved sharply to the left to counteract it and then smartly back to a point directly above the helicopter at precisely the moment that the movement stops. It is very difficult to draw this in an adequate manner, but Figure 67 may help.

A model helicopter behaves in exactly the same way. If the helicopter is moving, to stop it you must apply an opposite control movement and then remove it at the precise moment that the helicopter stops. The orientation simulator described earlier also works in this manner. This pendulum visualisation helped the writer considerably at the point where he was just about to master the hovering stage.

Trimming

One aspect we have not mentioned so far is the matter of model trim. Here again, experienced help is invaluable. A well-trimmed model is much easier to fly and it is difficult for the beginner to trim a model without help.

When steering the model around on the ground, in the zero height hover, it will soon be obvious if the model has a pronounced tendency to keep heading in one direction or turning one way and it is a simple matter to use the transmitter trim controls to correct this. Unfortunately, this trim correction may not be correct when the model leaves the ground. The solution here is to perform very short hops and observe the behaviour of the model. If the model repeatedly moves to the right, then left cyclic trim is needed and vice versa. If the model insists on moving forwards, then rear cyclic trim is needed, etc.

Tail rotor trim is variable and depends on many factors which are discussed elsewhere. At best this will always be a compromise – which explains why this is one of the most difficult aspects of learning to fly.

Now it's up to you

The writer has done his best to point out the difficulties and pitfalls associated with learning to hover but the truth is that from here on you are entirely on your own. Only the previously mentioned sheer dogged persistence will finally get you there. Be warned that once mastered, it is highly addictive.

11 First circuits

Tail-in circles

Having reached the point where you can hover the model consistently with its nose into wind and you standing behind it, you have established a 'safe base' position. Once you have become thoroughly familiar with this you can venture on to other things. Beware of becoming so fixated on this one position that you acquire a mental block against progressing further. This is a very real danger which can be very difficult to break out of.

Even while you are still becoming familiar with this position you do not have to stay frozen to one spot or direction. Try walking slowly round your flying field and taking the model with you. If it is calm there is no reason why you should not turn slowly round and walk back again. When there is a fair breeze blowing, walk very slowly backwards and take the model with you. Eventually you should be able to walk anywhere and everywhere with the model still in front of you.

From here it is a simple matter to turn slowly round and take the model round with you. The term 'tail-in circle' sounds terrifying to the beginner yet you have just done one! Easy, wasn't it? You will have noticed the recurrent use of the word 'slowly' by now – this is the whole secret of your early departures from the static hover condition. If you allow the speed to build up you will rapidly get into a situation you cannot cope with, so take it very steadily until you become more experienced and confident.

Confidence is very much another two-edged sword. You need it in order to make any progress, yet too much, too soon, can be disastrous. The maxim should be 'make haste – slowly'.

The tail-in circle is very easy in flat calm conditions and becomes progressively more difficult as the wind strength increases. In windy

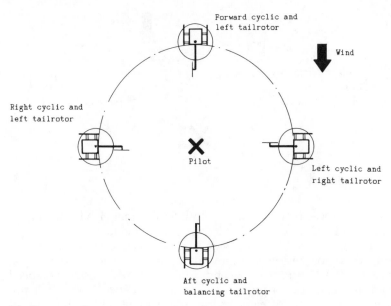

Forward cyclic and
left tailrotor

Wind

Right cyclic and
left tailrotor

X
Pilot

Left cyclic and
right tailrotor

Aft cyclic and
balancing tailrotor

Fig. 68 Trim offsets during tail-in circle.

conditions it is excellent practice in controlling the model even for the very experienced flyer. As the model presents different sides of itself to the wind, it is necessary to hold on various trim offsets to remain stationary (Figure 68) relative to the pilot. Your first attempts in a light breeze will probably get no further than the crosswind point. If things start to get out of control, turn the model into wind and move it forward to the 'safe' position.

The next stage is to let the model drift slowly backwards until it is hovering alongside you or, in calm conditions, turn it until it is sideways on. If you are an experienced fixed wing flyer, be warned that the latter course can be dangerous to you. Should the model start to move away, into wind, sideways, your natural inclination will be to pull the stick back to stop it. The helicopter will then back smartly into the ground!

There are two possible correct courses of action in this situation:

(a) Apply sideways cyclic to correct the movement, or, possibly better

(b) Apply tail rotor to turn the model back to the familiar hover position.

You will almost certainly find that you are happier to be seeing one side of the model than the other. Here again, don't let this

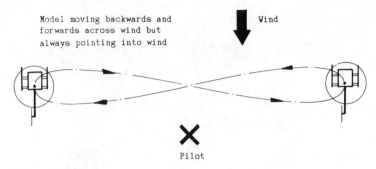

Fig. 69 Lazy eight.

situation develop until you can only fly the model on one side of you. Work at the 'bad' side until there is no difference.

Having got used to a side view, the next stage is to let the model drift slowly backwards and forwards across the wind in front of you (Figure 69). Starting very gently, you can increase both the speed and the sharpness of the turns as your confidence grows until you are flying a figure of eight course, still without letting the nose of the model point straight at you (Figure 70).

If you have any fixed wing experience, you will by now have realised a very important difference between helicopters and aeroplanes.

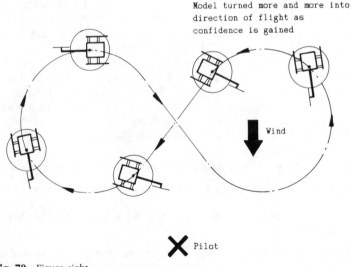

Fig. 70 Figure eight.

92

Two views of the Robbe *Ecureuil* (Squirrel) which uses Heim mechanics and a high-output 10 cc glow motor and is a good example of a modern scale model helicopter. The receiver aerial runs inside the fuselage rather than dangling beneath and risking snagging.

Turn with the rudder, not the elevator

When a full-sized aircraft is turned, the normal procedure is to apply a combination of rudder and aileron and then to use the elevator to maintain height. This results in a smooth 'co-ordinated' turn without any slipping or skidding. This, of course, is fine if you have an on-board pilot who can feel what is happening. With model aircraft, the usual method is to initiate a roll by use of the ailerons or the rudder/dihedral couple and then apply elevator to pull the model round. The result is an overbanked 'slipping' turn, but this is only apparent to the careful observer.

With a helicopter, however, the procedure is somewhat different. First, you must appreciate that a helicopter produces two different types of lift. Apart from the obvious lift produced by the rotors, which are revolving wings, there is another lift component produced by the rotor disc when moving forwards through the air (like a sort of flat, circular, wing). This is known as 'translational lift' and accounts for the fact that a helicopter requires less power to maintain height in forward flight than it does in the hover (Figure 71).

Now remember that a helicopter, unlike a conventional aircraft, does not necessarily have to be pointing in the direction that it is moving and that the pilot must tell the tail where to go at all times. Consider a helicopter which is flying forwards and about to make a turn. First we must use lateral cyclic (aileron) to produce a bank. This applies a sideways lift component which starts the model turning and we must immediately apply tail rotor (rudder) to make the fuselage follow the turn. The result of this is that the rotor disc shows a greater angle of incidence relative to the direction in which the model was originally travelling and, therefore, more lift (Figure 72).

This means that fore/aft cyclic (elevator) is not required and a turn is made with co-ordinated lateral cyclic and tail rotor (aileron/rudder). If the model is travelling at some speed and/or a sharp

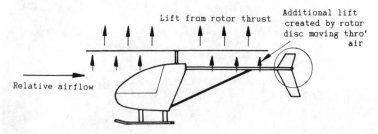

Fig. 71 Translational lift.

94

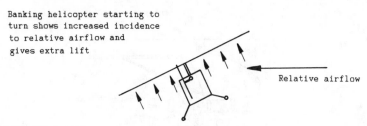

Banking helicopter starting to turn shows increased incidence to relative airflow and gives extra lift

Relative airflow

Fig. 72   Lift due to turn.

turn is made, it will in fact gain height despite the fact that no back cyclic is applied.

Be warned, however, that the story does not end there since helicopters display markedly different characteristics between right and left turns! Practise the above and familiarise yourself with the co-ordination required for turns in each direction before trying to fly proper circuits. This will reduce the possibility of unpleasant surprises.

Ground effect

Let's go back to the situation where the model is hovering in calm air. Below a height roughly equal to the diameter of the rotor, the model will be very lively and difficult to keep stationary due to interference between the ground and the downwash from the rotors. In effect, the model is balanced on a bubble of air and keeps trying to slide off it. Climb a little higher and things become much smoother because you are out of the so-called 'ground effect'.

In flat calm conditions, this effect can be clearly seen since the exhaust smoke will be observed to be blown away from the model by the rotors when out of ground effect (Figure 73), while it will

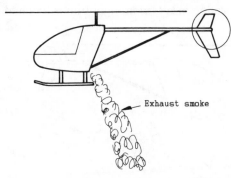

Exhaust smoke

Fig. 73   Out of ground effect.

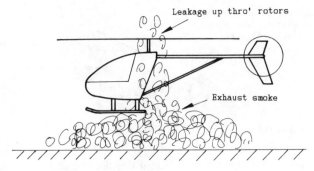

Fig. 74 In ground effect.

tend to form a cloud under the helicopter, or even 'leak' up through the middle of the rotors, when in ground effect (Figure 74).

If we now add a breeze to this situation, the bubble of air tends to be blown away from under the model and the effect occurs at a lower altitude (Figure 75). In a strong enough wind the effect is virtualy non-existent.

Another aspect of the calm air hover is that the tail has to be 'flown', or positioned, all the time, whereas a wind produces a 'weathercock' effect which makes things much easier. However, this weathercock effect influences the torque/tail rotor balance and results in a change of tail rotor trim.

Remember that the primary purpose of the tail rotor is to counteract the torque effect of the main rotor and maintain the fuselage at a constant heading. If we add our weathercock effect on to this, the tail rotor is now too effective and a trim change is required (Figure 76). This trim change will vary with wind strength. On a model with clockwise rotating rotors (viewed from the top) this will mean more left trim as the wind becomes stronger. Anticlockwise rotation means more right trim is required.

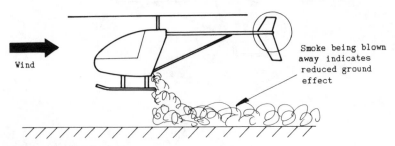

Fig. 75 Effect of wind on ground effect.

All of this means that hovering in a wind is rather easier since the ground effect is less marked and the tail is easier to control, despite a small trim change. Exactly the same situation applies when the model is flying forwards in calm, or windy, air.

One other aspect of hovering in a wind is that it will tend to mask any offset in the tail rotor trim. This offset will be easily detectable in calm air since the helicopter will turn slowly round. In a wind, however, the model will only turn until the trim offset is balanced by the weathercock effect. It will then maintain a constant heading at an angle to the wind. This effect is best corrected by observing the exhaust smoke and trimming the model so that the tail boom is pointing in the same direction that the smoke is being blown. If a gyro is fitted, this can tend to hide the effect of the trim offset and can, in gusty conditions, cause the tail to oscillate and lead to the mistaken conclusion that the gyro is too sensitive.

Other trim changes

Another, less known, effect of the tail rotor is that it requires a lateral cyclic trim offset to compensate for the sideways push which it applies (Figure 77). If we consider a machine with clockwise blade rotation, the tail rotor has to apply a push to the right side of the tail to cancel the torque reaction. Apart from preventing the helicopter from rotating about its vertical axis, this also makes the model drift to its left and requires some right cyclic trim to balance it. This trim offset is virtually constant and is not very dependent on forward speed.

In theory, some lateral trim should also be required when hovering in a wind, or flying forwards, to cancel out the additional lift produced by the forward travelling blade. In the writer's experience, however, this effect is negligible. It would, perhaps, be

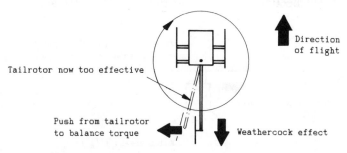

Fig. 76 Tail rotor trim change in wind.

significant on machines with low rotor speeds and is just noticeable when hovering tail to wind, which requires opposite trim offset.

Forward flight

Flying forwards is exactly the same as hovering in a wind except that we now have to consciously do things which we probably did automatically in the hover. First of all, some forward cyclic is needed to initiate the forward movement. Note that the word used was *initiate* – not *cause*. If you held on the forward stick the nose down attitude would increase and the model would move away from you at ever increasing speed and things would rapidly develop into an uncontrollable situation for the novice.

Forward cyclic is applied only long enough to produce a slight nose down attitude in the model. The fore/aft cyclic is then returned to neutral and the machine will accelerate up to a speed consistent with that attitude and stay there. For initial attempts it is best to apply only very short 'stabs' of cyclic control. If you practised walking around with the model in the hover you should have got the hang of this already. What you should try to remember is that a helicopter is essentially a frictionless device and, once moving, will tend to continue moving until an opposite command is given to stop it. From this it follows that if a given command is held on, the result is a steadily increasing speed.

Once the machine starts to move, there will be a loss of lift due to the sideways force being used to produce the movement and more power will be required. However, this effect is only temporary since, once moving, the already described translational lift will produce a gain in altitude unless power is reduced.

Now that the machine is moving (remember – not too fast at first) you should notice the change in tail rotor trim. Face up to the fact now that you simply cannot keep altering the trim to suit every speed or situation that you may encounter. You must learn to 'fly the tail' all the time by using the rudder stick. After all, you are

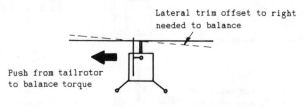

Fig. 77   Lateral trim offset due to tail rotor.

98

using proportional radio gear, are you not? Make the dog wag the tail rather than the other way round. Eventually you will reach the point where you will wonder why one thumb appears to be getting tired and will look down to find that you were holding on a lot of stick trim without even being aware of it!

This trim change will be very noticeable on early, fixed pitch machines, less noticeable on collective models and, possibly, almost non-existent on the latest designs. Some early designs incorporated fin offset in an attempt to combat it, with varying success.

At this stage it might be a good idea to consider ways of stopping the beast!

If you can't stop, put it sideways

No, we have not switched to lecture on rally driving. Your helicopter is moving forwards and you want to stop it. Easy, you say, apply back cyclic. Well, yes, it can be that easy if you are only moving fairly slowly, but bear in mind that to stop in a reasonable distance you have to hold on the control long enough to raise the nose and apply a braking force. When the machine stops, you must immediately lower the nose and increase the power to the hover level. If the model is travelling at some speed, things become much more complicated. Raising the nose will cause an increase in translational lift and make the helicopter climb – possibly quite sharply. To avoid this you must reduce power yet be ready to level out and increase power when the motion stops – not easy for the novice.

Fortunately, there is an easier, if rather untidy, way which you have already learned if you did the figure eights across wind which were suggested earlier. Simply apply lateral cyclic and tail rotor commands to bank and turn the model so that it presents its side view to the direction of travel. The resulting sharp increase in drag will provide a rapid deceleration and far less sideways cyclic will be required to provide braking effort. If you overdo it, the model will merely slip sideways, which is much easier to control than a tail down reversal into the ground. You may by now have learned that this is probably the most expensive way to crash!

To sum up all of the above in one sentence, remember – cyclic controls speed, throttle controls height.

Circuit and see

Now, at last, we come to your first true circuit. There are two ways of flying a circuit with a helicopter (at least!). The first is what might be termed the 'fixed wing' approach. By this we mean large

Robert Gorham demonstrates the 'party trick' of inverted flying with his GMP *Competitor*. Modern electronics has simplified control but ground effect on a rotor six inches from the grass is considerable and only very experienced pilots can attempt such low level stunts.

fast circuits similar to those flown by a conventional aircraft. Secondly, we have the slow, close in type of circuit which is much more characteristic of a helicopter.

Graduates from fixed wing models will find the first type the most natural way to go but they can become dangerous if you get into trouble or become disorientated. In this situation you will automatically revert to those fixed wing reflexes which you spent so much time in developing and they can lead you sadly astray! Nonetheless, this is probably the best way to go for that first circuit whether you have any previous model flying experience or not.

If you used floats on your model during the initial learning period and have since removed them, it would be well worth replacing them for your first circuits. For one thing they will limit the forward speed which can be developed. They will also aid orientation and allow the model to be landed safely while still moving (in any direction!) which is not true of a model equipped with skids. If you find yourself in the position of having to land the model some distance away (which you will), here again they will be of great help.

Right, we can't delay it any longer. Starting from a stable hover, push in some forward cyclic and add some throttle. Don't bother to reduce power as the model accelerates, let it climb. You will notice that the model tends to yaw to the right (on clockwise rotors) and fly crabwise. When you become more proficient, you may want to re-trim; at this stage correct it with the stick since this will help to reduce problems during the more difficult slowing down phase.

Having travelled a reasonable distance into wind (you did wait three years for a day with a light breeze, didn't you?) apply some sideways cyclic to bank the model and start a turn. Avoid any tendency to pull the model round with back cyclic: this should not be necessary and will rob you of forward speed which is not advisable at this stage. What will be necessary, however, is to use the tail rotor to keep the fuselage pointing in the direction of travel.

A common fault here is to think of the rotor disc as being the model and watch it describe a graceful turn only to find that the fuselage is now pointing its tail at the ground. At this point, you will either slide backwards into the ground (no, the model, stupid) or execute a neat stall turn and dig a hole with the nose! Now you know why I advised you to let it climb.

This situation is complicated by the fact that the majority of models have clockwise rotating rotors and most pilots are right-handed. By a quirk of human nature most right-handed pilots want to turn left (it's all in the mind), while your clockwise rotating, forward flying, helicopter is still stubbornly trying to yaw to the right (Figure 78). QED. You could, of course, defy convention and make all your early turns to the right. What this all boils down to is that if you make a turn to the left while flying forwards at high speed with clockwise blade rotation you will probably need to apply full left tail rotor. Some models are worse than others in this respect due to variations in fin area, tail rotor disc area and about 573 other variables.

Assuming that you manage to complete your first 180° turn and are now starting a down wind leg, use lateral cyclic to roll the model back to level flight. Remember that you need to hold some tail rotor on to fly straight. If you forget, the helicopter will resume flying crabwise and give you a fairly gentle reminder.

I do not intend, now or ever, to become involved in any controversy about downwind turns, but when making downwind turns with a helicopter you should ensure that your ground speed downwind is faster than the wind speed (Figure 79). You can easily get into a situation where the model is flying forwards relative to the ground but is actually flying backwards through the air. This is an unstable condition and the model will attempt to turn through 180° to face the direction of the airflow. The effect to the pilot is that the model has just made a half turn and proceeded to fly backwards (Figure 80). While you are confused prepare yourself for a chat with your bank manager!

In case of emergency
This is a good point to consider what you should do in this kind of emergency. If you are in any way doubtful about what is happening, or are disorientated or confused, the first rule of model helicopter flying is to add power and go up. Believe it or not,

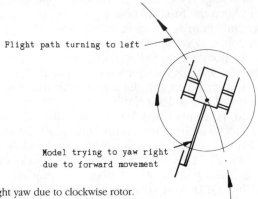

Flight path turning to left

Model trying to yaw right due to forward movement

Fig. 78   Right yaw due to clockwise rotor.

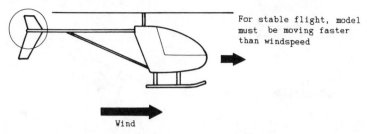

For stable flight, model
must be moving faster
than windspeed

Wind

Fig. 79 Keep groundspeed higher than airspeed.

height is not dangerous to this type of model! I have seen choppers almost totally destroyed from a height of less than 3 inches, yet have seen many crashes which started at 100 feet, or more, and produced only minimal damage. Don't be afraid of altitude, it buys you a very useful commodity – time.

If the model is rotating, or apparently flying backwards, or you are in any doubt about what it is doing, apply some forward cyclic. This should make the model start to move in the direction which it is pointing or stop the rotation. If the rotation is due to something having broken on the model, you have another problem which we will discuss in a later chapter. Now, back to our circuit.

Having completed your downwind leg, you now make another turn to bring the model back into wind. This introduces another danger (you guessed!) if your airspeed after the turn is not higher than the wind speed. The model may now be facing you and flying forwards through the air yet be stationary, or flying backwards, relative to the ground. You are not ready for the nose-in hover at this stage, so some other remedy is required.

The writer's solution to this problem during early circuits was to deliberately make a steep slipping turn into wind to ensure a high airspeed (Figure 81). A slight reduction of power before starting the turn helps to produce a higher rate of descent. This can

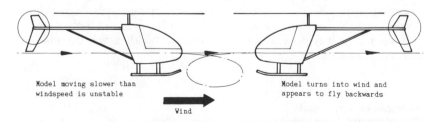

Model moving slower than
windspeed is unstable

Wind

Model turns into wind and
appears to fly backwards

Fig. 80 Effect of insufficient airspeed downwind.

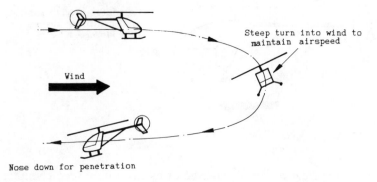

Steep turn into wind to maintain airspeed

Wind

Nose down for penetration

Fig. 81 Steep turn into wind to maintain speed.

develop into a bad habit later so you should work away at producing a more controlled turn and slow steady flight into wind.

Now say 'back a bit!'

So, the model is now flying back towards you, into wind, and you have to bring it down, slow it down and get back into the hover position. Reduce power enough to ensure a rate of descent which will bring the model down to ground level just in front of you. If too great a reduction is required, go round again and start the descent further away (careful), or lower. This part is much easier if the model is equipped with an autorotation freewheel, but that, too, we will cover later.

As the model approaches the ground, start applying back cyclic to produce a flare, without adding power. Do not add power, or release the back stick, until the model stops moving forwards. If in doubt, add power and forward stick and go round again. If you get it right, the model will maintain constant height, with reducing airspeed and increasingly nose high attitude until it stops. Push the nose down, add hover power and there you are (Figure 82). Assuming that you have plenty of fuel left, immediately increase power and do another circuit to gain confidence and prove to yourself that it was no fluke. This confidence building will become increasingly important from now on.

A negative approach

The descent from high speed forward flight is an aspect of helicopter flying which many fliers find to be very difficult. There

104

Mike Young's *Morley* MXA, a general purpose/trainer design for .40 size motors. Much use is made of plastics in its construction and the main side frames are simple flat aluminium plates. Also available is the MXA Plus which is fully aerobatic.

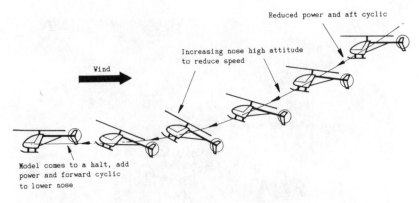

Reduced power and aft cyclic

Increasing nose high attitude
to reduce speed

Wind

Model comes to a halt, add
power and forward cyclic
to lower nose

Fig. 82   Flare and return to hover.

are several ways in which the process can be made both easier and safer.

So far, the model has been set up in such a way that the pitch of the main blades is always positive. Things can now be made very much easier by the introduction of some negative pitch. Up till now we have avoided this to reduce the risk of the blades striking the boom during the process of learning to hover. When you have reached the stage of flying circuits this risk should have disappeared due to your being able to perform gentle landings and exercise the necessary throttle control.

By now arranging things so that the blades go down to $-1\frac{1}{2}°$ to $-2°$ when the throttle is fully closed a landing approach can be made with the blades at zero, or slightly negative pitch, but still at a moderate throttle setting to give full control.

Another way of achieving this same situation is by use of the 'idle up' switch on your transmitter. This function is more fully described elsewhere but the idea is to artificially raise the idle speed when the throttle stick is pulled right back.

If the model is equipped with an autorotation freewheel, this may be used in conjunction with negative pitch to allow very steep descents to be made with the throttle fully closed. This is more fully discussed in a later chapter.

Bad habits

When you begin to fly your model in circuits regularly, do be sure to practise both right and left hand circuits to avoid building up a bias towards one particular direction. We have already mentioned that right-handed pilots seem to have a natural tendency to turn left. It is very easy to get into the habit of making all of your turns to the left and a point will be reached where you will be very reluctant to turn right. When you do reach this point the fact that most model helicopters have different handling characteristics between right and left hand turns will make matters even worse.

It cannot be repeated too often – don't develop a bias towards one particular attitude or direction.

12 Advanced circuits

Orientation

Having reached the point of flying your model around in circuits, rather like a fixed wing model, you will sooner or later – probably sooner – arrive at a point where you are unsure of the model's exact position or attitude. There are many variations of this situation ranging from a momentary doubt all the way up to total disorientation followed by loss of control and a crash.

The model helicopter pilot is not alone in suffering from this problem. Fixed wing model flyers have to go through this same situation during the learning stages. However, whereas a conventional model will tend to go on flying, the model helicopter needs to be flown all the time and the risk of a crash due to disorientation is much greater.

Curiously enough, the problem does not relate to the quality of the pilot's eyesight. It does not matter how well you may be able to see the model if you are unable to relate the information in terms of the action required. For this reason it is undoubtedly true that the problem becomes less as you become more experienced and will eventually disappear.

This is small comfort to those who are currently crashing models due to becoming disorientated, however, so let's see what can be done to help matters.

(1) Make more of the model visible. The writer has found it to be a great help if the main rotor blades are covered with a glossy white material. In sunlight the rotor disc becomes visible and this gives more information on the roll attitude of the model. A model helicopter is a very narrow object and

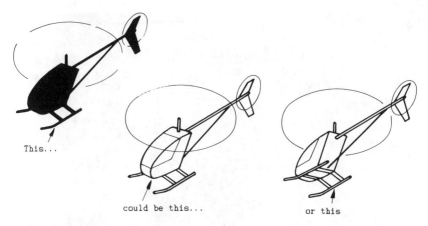

This...

could be this...

or this

Fig. 83 Disorientation in silhouette.

unless the disc can be seen the only indication of whether the model is banked or level comes from observation of the undercarriage skids. Figure 83 indicates the type of situation we are considering. Figure 84 shows the effect of making the disc visible. In poor light, the effect is much less marked but there is still more of the disc visible, particularly if the model is against some background other than the sky.

(2) The above two figures also indicate the difficulty which can be experienced in discerning whether the model is coming towards you or going away. This is a more difficult problem to solve, but, assuming that the model is a pod and boom type, one solution is to paint the nose cowling a highly visible colour. Many people see one particular colour far better than others and, if this is so in your case, this is the

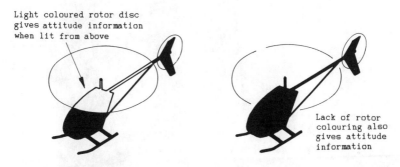

Light coloured rotor disc gives attitude information when lit from above

Lack of rotor colouring also gives attitude information

Fig. 84 Silhouette plus disc.

Plastics are playing an increasing part in model helicopter kit manufacture. This is the Morley *Hughes 300* for .40cc.in. (6½cc) motors, which is of largely plastic construction.

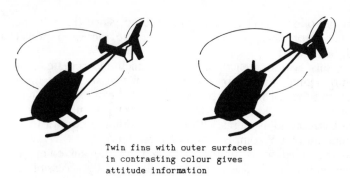

Twin fins with outer surfaces
in contrasting colour gives
attitude information

Fig. 85   Tailplane with twin fins.

colour to paint your pod. With this type the remainder of the
model is usually predominantly black, which means that if
you can see lots of colour it must be coming towards you!

(3) Model shape can be a help too. Some designs (notably the
Hirobo range) feature a horizontal stabiliser with twin fins
(Figure 85). This can help to give both roll and direction
information, particularly if the fins are painted different
colours on the inner and outer faces.

(4) When you have enough experience to have reached the
stage where crashes are a rare occurrence (if ever!), the
greatest aid to orientation is to fit a scale type fuselage –
there are very few freelance fuselages – to your model. This
is invariably wider and deeper which is a great help. The
greater cost and effort involved in repairing it probably helps
to reduce the risks taken too!

High speed flight

When you are competent at flying your model around like a fixed
wing aircraft, you will find that you are using more and more
power until you reach a point where the throttle is fully open. The
model is now flying at the maximum speed of which it is capable
and is in a situation where all power above that required to
maintain height goes into making the model move forwards. This
means that the model will be in a marked nose down attitude
(Figure 86).

In this situation, several of the trim balances – and compromises
– become considerably changed. Tail rotor trim certainly becomes
very complex under these conditions. We have already seen that the
weathercock effect due to forward flight makes the tail rotor too
effective. This is further complicated if a helicopter radio with some

111

form of collective/tail rotor mixing is used, since this will increase the tail rotor pitch to compensate for the increased power and pitch being used.

For this reason, helicopter radios which incorporate a second idle-up setting ('idle up 2') will usually have some means of modifying the tail rotor response when this feature is selected. This is achieved by switching in a new set of 'up' and 'down' compensation adjustments (*JR* sets), or adding a control to reduce the amount of 'up' compensation (*Futaba* sets).

Another method is simply to switch off the tail compensation system and some radios are fitted with an easily accessible switch for this purpose.

At high speeds the fore/aft cyclic response becomes very critical in some designs. In the writer's opinion there is a definite relationship between the size and incidence angle of the horizontal stabiliser (tailplane) and the angle of the mainshaft (some designs have the shaft raked forwards). However, this relationship has not so far been sufficiently investigated to ensure that a given design will be stable in fast forward flight. Not all authorities agree on this point and many experienced fliers maintain that the horizontal stabiliser is unnecessary.

The most common problem to be experienced is that the model porpoises or is excessively sensitive to elevator input. Another common trait is for the model to pitch up as speed increases, making it difficult, if not impossible, to maintain a shallow dive as an entry to an aerobatic manoeuvre. Any free play or slop in the fore/aft cyclic linkages will only make this situation worse. Some designs are far better than others regarding the linkages associated with this control. Systems which employ two pushrods to the swashplate – one in front and one behind – are the ones to look for.

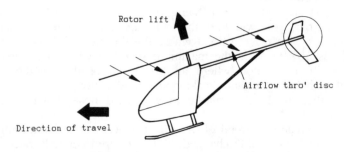

Rotor lift

Airflow thro' disc

Direction of travel

Model nose down to produce high forward speed

Fig. 86 High speed forward flight.

High speed descent

With increasing speed the previously described difficulties associated with descent and translation back to hovering flight become more acute. It may be found that the model will not descend at all unless a considerable amount of negative pitch is available.

While you can, of course, slow the model down before beginning a descent, there will still be problems if you fly in windy weather. Even if the model is flying slowly relative to the ground, its airspeed may still be quite high. Here again the more advanced radios cater for this situation by incorporating a separate low pitch adjustment associated with the 'idle up 2' function. By this means it is possible to have more negative pitch than usual (say −5°) when required.

The whole subject of high speed forward flight will become of increased importance when you attempt to perform aerobatics, as described in a later chapter.

13 Advanced hovering

Slow circuits

Any manoeuvre, or circuit, which your model may perform while travelling fairly slowly may be considered as an advanced hovering manoeuvre. Here the model is not subject, to any significant degree, to the trim changes or translational lift effects which occur during fast forward flight.

We have already considered the tail-in circle, which can be performed in either direction. The same manoeuvre can be performed with the model sideways on to you and travelling forwards (Figure 87), or backwards (Figure 88), again in either direction.

So far, we have only considered circles around the pilot. The next step is to perform a circle, or circuit, off to one side (Figure 89). This is something which many fliers find to be extremely difficult and here, as before, the longer you delay the more difficult it becomes. There is no easy solution to this one other than doing the first ones at a safe altitude, which means at some speed since it is difficult to fly slowly at any height or distance.

From this point you can progressively reduce both the height and the speed until the model is performing very slow circles just above the ground. This can take a very long time to accomplish, however, and will bring you closer and closer to the next stage to be conquered.

The nose-in hover

Having spent a great deal of time on learning to hover in the 'safe base' position, a point will be reached where your carefully acquired reflexes begin to work against you. When the model is

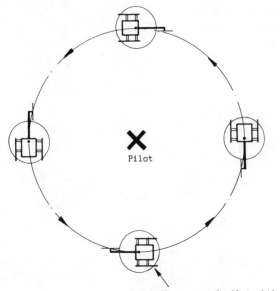

Model flown around pilot while
presenting constant side view

Fig. 87 Forwards circle.

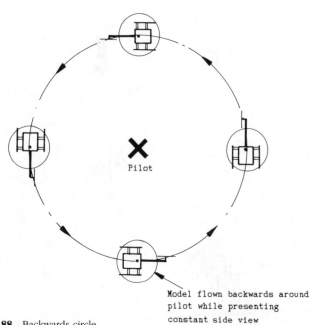

Model flown backwards around
pilot while presenting
constant side view

Fig. 88 Backwards circle.

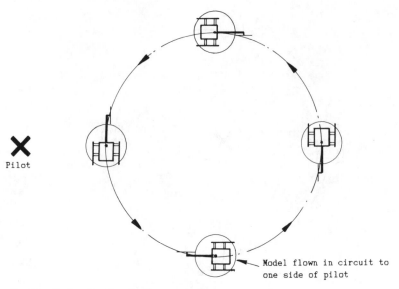

Model flown in circuit to
one side of pilot

Fig. 89 Circle with pilot outside.

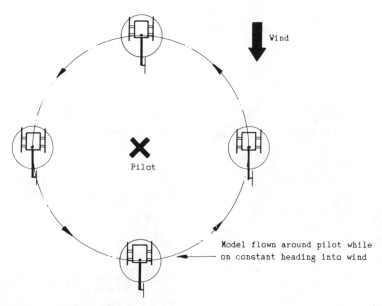

Wind

Model flown around pilot while
on constant heading into wind

Fig. 90 Constant heading circle.

116

facing you instead of pointing away from you, the fore/aft and lateral cyclic controls will appear to be reversed. It is very difficult to make this transition and there are many varied ways which have been suggested to help in the initial stages.

Our previously described orientation trainer can be a great help to some in this situation, but others have difficulty in relating the trainer to a real model helicopter.

If you can fly the model around in circuits you will have already reached the point where you can fly the model towards you, a situation which will present no problems to experienced fixed wing fliers. However, when you try to stop the model in that position the whole situation seems suddenly to change and things can rapidly reach a point of total confusion. In this situation it seems to be a natural reaction to pull in back cyclic which leads to the model reversing away from you. Remember the cardinal rule in this situation is to push both sticks forward, but do be ready to leap out of the way if necessary!

Practise flying the model towards you at slower and slower speed – and at a safe height – with short stops at frequent intervals. Curiously enough, the writer found that if this is done in a fairly strong, but steady, wind, it is possible to visualise the model as flying forwards even when it is stationary relative to the ground! It is also easier to stop the forward movement in this situation since many models require a positive effort to make headway against anything more than a stiff breeze.

Should you get into difficulties during this situation a better method of recovery would be to execute a half turn with the tail rotor control and allow the model to head off downwind. It can then be turned back into wind for another attempt.

Another method of learning to hover with the model facing you is to place it on the ground in this attitude and learn to fly again from scratch. This is a very frustrating approach, however, and you will be constantly tempted to turn the model round and get on with some real flying.

The final move is to turn around taking the model with you, as before, and you will be performing one of the most difficult of all hovering manoeuvres – the nose-in circle.

Pirouettes

In its simplest form this manoeuvre consists of placing the model in a stable hover and applying full left or right tail rotor command. In theory the model should rotate about its vertical axis until the control is released and then stop. If the model should decide to rotate of its own accord due to something having broken it will

117

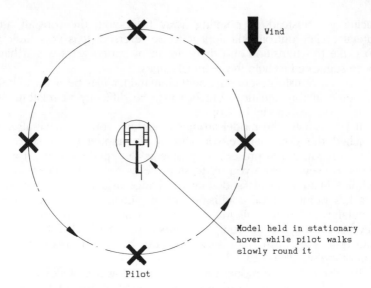

Wind

Model held in stationary
hover while pilot walks
slowly round it

Pilot

Fig. 91 Promenade.

usually stay in one spot and rotate quite happily. When the same
thing is attempted deliberately, however, one turn is usually enough
to send the model shooting off at great speed in some totally
unexpected direction!

Once again we return to the old advice to practise at a safe
height. If rate switches are in use, they should be set in the
low position since difficulties are usually pilot-induced
(unintentionally) and it helps to make the model as docile as
possible. Many models require some lateral cyclic input to assist in
making a stable turn. This is usually – but not always – in the same
direction as the tail rotor command.

Constant heading circle

We can combine the pirouette with our hovering circuit by turning
around and taking the model around too, as before, but with the
model always pointing into wind (Figure 90). Thus the model
performs a slow pirouette relative to the pilot while turning around
the pilot. If you are close to mastering the slow pirouette, you may
find this to be easier since the model is always pointing into wind.

Another variation on this is to hover the model at a constant
heading and walk slowly round it (Figure 91). This manoeuvre is
known as a pilot's promenade.

118

The Heim *Bell 222* is sleek and cleans up neatly with retractable landing gear. K. Lancaster's model is powered by an OS 61 FSR. Exhaust smoke, as clearly visible in the photo below, can be a very useful flight aid at times.

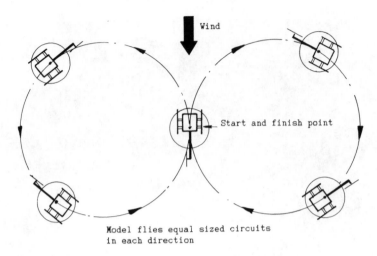

Wind

Start and finish point

Model flies equal sized circuits
in each direction

Fig. 92   Horizontal eight.

The horizontal eight

This is not to be confused with our old friend the lazy eight, described earlier. It is a true figure eight circuit flown at slow speed in front of the pilot (Figure 92) and forms one of the compulsory manoeuvres flown in FAI contests. Most authorities agree that it is possibly the most difficult of all the hovering manoeuvres and it combines the difficulties of both the nose-in hover and the pirouette. In contests it has to be flown over four marker flags which makes it even more difficult.

If you have become fairly proficient at the nose-in hover you may find that this figure is easier to perform by standing with your back to the wind and taking off and landing in the nose-in position. This makes the figure identical to our old friend the lazy eight where the nose of the model does not actually cross the pilot's eye-line.

The FAI schedule contains several other similar optional manoeuvres which are described in Appendix 5.

Autorotation

14

The right pitch

Strictly speaking there are two types of autorotation: as a safety device aimed at landing the model in one piece after an engine failure or as an aerobatic manoeuvre. The difference is that in the former it does not matter where the model is landed – as long as the area is clear of people and property – or how untidy the landing is, while in the latter case it must look good and land on a small spot.

Basically, the autorotation descent is performed by reducing the pitch of the main blades to a negative figure – typically −2° to −3° – so that the blades will continue to rotate while the model is in an engine-off descent. The actual amount of pitch used is quite critical and controls the 'glide' angle. Too much negative will give a very rapid descent with high blade speed, while insufficient negative will give a shallow glide with low rotor RPM. It may be difficult to imagine the concept of a helicopter 'gliding' but this is an accurate description of the process since it is directly comparable to a gliding fixed wing model. With a fixed wing machine the forward movement is caused by the descent and care must be taken to keep the airspeed up to avoid stalling. With a helicopter the rotation is caused by the descent and the blade speed must be maintained to avoid a 'stall' and loss of control.

The analogy can be carried even further if we consider what happens as we approach the stall. With an aircraft the nose can be raised and the angle of attack increased until the model is flying very slowly but not quite stalling. Similarly we can reduce the negative pitch of the blades – and even go slightly positive – without the blades actually stopping. However, this is a dangerous situation since there will be insufficient energy in the system to land the model. From this we can see that it is possible to control both the rate and angle of descent by varying the pitch (Figure 93). However, this does need lots of practice to get right.

There will be one optimum pitch setting which gives the maximum blade RPM and this is the ideal point to aim for when setting up the model. Note that the word used is 'ideal' rather than correct, since the correct pitch may be influenced by other factors. The correct pitch for any model can only be determined by experiment which is why experienced contest fliers prefer to have too much negative and 'fly the pitch' on the way down. If you are only interested in autorotation as a means of saving the model in the event of an engine failure the pitch can simply be set to the manufacturer's recommended figure (or, if in doubt $-2\frac{1}{2}°$). However, it must be stressed that you must still practise the manoeuvre if you are to stand any chance of success.

Freewheel or clutch

So far we have not considered the effect of an autorotation clutch on the model. This device should more accurately be described as a freewheel, the intent of which is to allow the blades to rotate at high speed while the motor is idling or stopped. While this condition will exist anyway as soon as the clutch has disengaged, there are good reasons for allowing the rotor to rotate freely. It takes a measurable time for the motor to decelerate to the point where the clutch disengages and during this time it will tend to

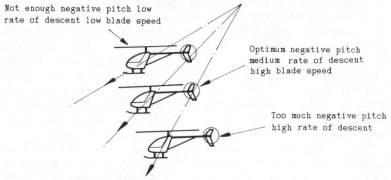

Not enough negative pitch low rate of descent low blade speed

Optimum negative pitch medium rate of descent high blade speed

Too much negative pitch high rate of descent

Fig. 93 Effect of pitch on glide angle.

Another model making extensive use of plastics is the Hirobo *Shuttle*, which comes ready-assembled with a .28 cu.in. (4.6 cc) motor already installed. A case of 'just add radio' and you're ready to fly!

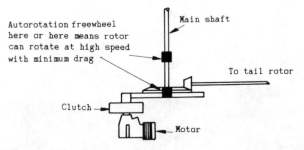

Autorotation freewheel
here or here means rotor
can rotate at high speed
with minimum drag

Main shaft

To tail rotor

Clutch

Motor

Fig. 94 Position of autorotation clutch.

slow the rotor, which is undesirable. Another reason is that without such a freewheel, the tail rotor will continue to rotate at a normal speed and attempt to cancel out a torque effect which is no longer present.

This means that without a freewheel the result is an unwanted yawing effect which makes the landing more difficult, particularly if tail rotor/collective pitch mixing is being used. This mixing increases the tail rotor pitch to compensate for the increased torque when collective pitch is added, but in an autorotation landing there is no torque at all so the yaw effect is even more pronounced. To combat this the freewheel is normally positioned in the main gearwheel which drives the rotor shaft (Figure 94) and the result is that the tail rotor slows with the motor and actually stops when the clutch disengages. This does mean, of course, that there is no control over the model's yaw axis (rudder to you fixed wing fliers) during the descent, although the natural weathercock effect of the fuselage will keep it lined up in the direction of flight.

One other benefit of fitting the freewheel in the main gear is that

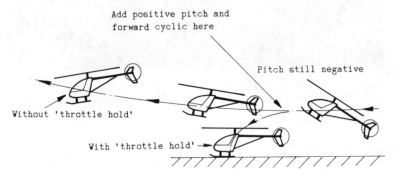

Add positive pitch and
forward cyclic here

Pitch still negative

Without 'throttle hold'

With 'throttle hold'

Fig. 95 Autorotation flare.

124

the rotor is not encumbered by the rest of the drive train, including the various reduction gears and tail drive, and is allowed to spin much more freely than would otherwise be the case.

Now land it!

Well, now, your helicopter is approaching the ground at a great rate of knots with the engine idling and you have to land it – gently. It used to be thought that the correct technique was to add positive pitch at just the right moment to give a survivable – if not gentle – landing. On very early model helicopters this was probably the only method which stood any chance of success, but only just! Both then and now it is a very difficult approach which requires very accurate timing.

With modern designs, the correct method is to make the descent with some forward speed and then use this speed to flare like an aircraft, still holding a negative pitch setting (Figure 95). In this way the model can be brought to a halt a short distance from the ground with all of the blade energy and pitch range still available to make the landing. Even if you make a complete mess of it the model only has a few inches to fall. The biggest danger is that of applying too much pitch at this point, causing the model to gain height again while dissipating all the useful blade energy. Another effect of the flare is to wind up the blade speed which helps to give a greater safety margin.

First attempts should be made by starting from a safe height and closing the throttle fully – don't use the 'throttle hold' switch at this

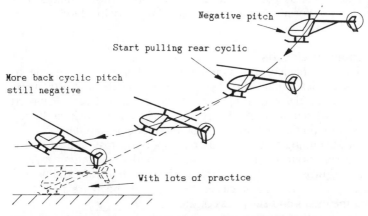

Note this and illustration opposite form one continual flight path.

125

stage. If the model is set up correctly it should make a steep descent under full control. You should see the tail rotor slow right down or even stop. While still at a safe height, apply back cyclic to flare the model into level flight and simultaneously add power to return to the hover position. Practise this until you can bring the model to a stop, in the hover, a few inches from the ground and just in front of you. If you are a fixed wing flier this part should be fairly easy!

Now comes the most difficult part, go and do it again but with the 'throttle hold' switched on as the model starts to descend. If the 'hold' is set to give a safe idle there should still be plenty of time to switch it off and recover even if you make a complete mess of things. The difficulty lies in convincing yourself of that! If all is well it will be simply a matter of lowering the model gently to the ground from the low level hover position. It really is that simple since you have already conquered the difficult part – the descent and flare.

It can be quite difficult to find the nerve (it can be quite difficult to find the switch too) to do your first 'full-down autorotation' (a descriptive American term). Mine occurred one day when the tail drive failed while flying around at a fair height. I can remember thinking 'Well, you know what to do – do it!' and the next thing I knew the model was safely on the ground. Fortunately I did remember to flick the hold switch on the way down. My first thought was, 'if it's that easy, what is all the fuss about?' I'm still trying to do another one half as good as the first one!

Some models will drop very rapidly during the early part of the descent while the main rotor winds up to a suitable speed. A trick used in FAI F3C contests is to use the 'idle up' switch to give a high blade RPM as the throttle is closed. Using this technique it is possible to perform a safe autorotation from a very low level.

Autorotation circuits

With lots of practice and increasing confidence it is possible to steer the model around the sky quite a lot on the way down. By banking the model and using back cyclic the model can be turned rather like a fixed wing model. The tail will 'weathercock' and keep the nose pointing in the direction that the model is travelling.

When attempting to land on a small spot you may indeed find it easier to start your autorotation with the model heading away from you in a downwind direction and perform a 180° turn during the descent. This can make it easier to arrive at the correct spot by varying the radius and steepness of the turn.

Finally, to return to an earlier point, while an autorotation landing can be used as a method of safely landing a model which has a dead engine, or some other problem, it does need practice. So, even if you don't intend to compete in FAI contests where it is necessary to perform smooth, polished, engine-off landings in a small box, why not have a go at doing some untidy, but gentle, ones somewhere in the same field?

15 Aerobatics

R/C set-up

When you decide that you wish to try flying aerobatics with your helicopter you should give serious thought to the degree of commitment that you are willing to make to your sport/hobby. While not absolutely essential, a helicopter radio will make things much easier – which probably means less expensive in the long run!

If you are still using a standard radio system and only wish to execute the odd loop or roll, then you can continue with your existing equipment, but you should realise that you are not going to be able to perform round loops or axial rolls. Even the best aerobatic helicopter/pilot combination available will not be able to perform these manoeuvres without some help from purpose designed radio equipment.

Assuming that you decide that you wish to take things seriously and intend to acquire suitable equipment you should look for a helicopter radio which has two idle-up systems, plus a throttle hold switch, with separate collective pitch adjustments on each. These will be used to set things up for three separate flight conditions:

(1) Hovering manoeuvres – Idle up 1.
(2) Aerobatic manoeuvres – Idle up 2.
(3) Autorotation – Throttle hold.

Idle up 1

This should be used to adjust the model in a manner similar to that which you have been used to so far. However, as we now have another set-up available for aerobatics the model can be made less sensitive. Normally the rate switches will be set in the 'low' position and, if variable gyro sensitivity is available, this will be set in the 'high' position. Only a small amount of negative pitch will be used.

The object here is to make the model fly as smoothly as possible and, ideally, the control movements should be set to the absolute minimum, while the gyro gain should be as high as possible. As the main object is to obtain a smooth hover, the actual idle-up controls should be set to give as nearly as possible a constant engine speed.

Remember that switching off both idle-up functions will give you normal throttle control for starting. It is essential that you check that this has been done before attempting to start the engine, otherwise a nasty accident could result.

Idle up 2

All of the settings used here have to be established in flight and most will be the result of some compromise or other. Rate switches will normally be set to the 'high' position, with the gyro sensitivity on the 'low' setting. The amount of negative pitch needed may, in extreme cases, be as much as the amount of positive pitch available (see later).

Control throws need to be sufficient to perform the manoeuvres required – which with some models means as much as possible. However, do try to avoid using too much movement as this will make the model 'twitchy' and cause excessive speed loss during manoeuvres.

Gyro gain depends on the individual flier. The gyro could be dispensed with when the model is in fast forward flight and can, if too powerful, actually hinder the performance of some manoeuvres. Most fliers prefer to retain some gyro effect but this will normally be a lower value than in the purely hovering mode.

Throttle should be set so that normal hovering RPM is maintained when the throttle/pitch stick is pulled right back to give full negative pitch.

Throttle hold

As previously explained this will put the throttle servo into a preset position while still allowing the pitch to be controlled by the throttle stick. For autorotation practice the throttle will be set to give a safe idle speed. In contest flying, the motor must be stopped and the throttle servo will be set to a position which achieves this. One or two helicopter radios are equipped with a second throttle hold option to allow the practice setting to be retained.

The KKK *Fox*, for .050-.061 cu.in. (8-10cc) engines is a fully aerobatic pod and boom design.

Pitch will be set to a negative figure which is suitable for an autorotation descent. Normally, any limiting adjustment which may have been made to the amount of positive pitch available will be over-ridden by this control. This ensures that the maximum amount of pitch is available for landing.

A halfway approach

If you are only interested in performing aerobatics on a casual basis and don't want to make the investment involved in one of the more advanced helicopter radios then one of the more generally available – and cheaper – sets with only one idle-up switch can be used. Here the idle-up facility will be used to set the model up for aerobatics and the normal throttle action used for general flying.

Are you sure you are ready?

As with all the stages so far discussed, during the process of learning to fly aerobatics the model will be put into many very unfamiliar positions and attitudes so it is essential that your flying capabilities are such that you are not still finding yourself in a position where you are disorientated. Are you still finding yourself in a condition where the model is sitting quite happily in the hover some distance away, but you are reluctant to apply some control input for fear of doing the wrong thing? If so, this is the exact thing that you must work at until you are happy that you can cope.

One thing which will cause problems in attempting any aerobatics is an underpowered helicopter. With aircraft you can start at considerable height and dive to gain speed. An underpowered helicopter will rapidly decelerate as soon as you apply any control input and the model will come to a dead stop – probably inverted. Now is the time to replace that tired old engine and, while you are at it, give the model a thorough check over too.

The loop

To most people aerobatics means 'looping the loop' and this is where we shall begin with our helicopter aerobatics. Just about every collective pitch helicopter available should be capable of performing this manoeuvre, but some are more capable than others. If you have any doubts about your particular model, then you should consult the manufacturers, importers, specialist shop, or local expert for advice on the subject.

Assuming that you are happy with your ability to cope with a helicopter in an unfamiliar attitude and with the mechanical soundness of your model, all you really need to do is to get the model up to a safe height, build up lots of forward speed, pull the cyclic stick back and watch it go round. It will probably be very untidy (and you may need that ability to cope with unfamiliar attitudes) but we are not concerned at this stage with what it looks like, only what it does.

Helicopters differ widely in their reaction to high forward speed. Some become more responsive with increasing speed, others less responsive. This does not only vary from make to make but between individual machines of the same make. I have seen a *Hirobo 808* which would loop from the hover, while another identical machine would not. Some idea of your particular model's handling characteristics can be gleaned from doing steep stall turns but eventually you will have to try a proper loop and see what happens. What you should not do at this stage is to listen to various people's advice on how to do precise round loops. Just go ahead and do sloppy, untidy, figure nines and get used to the idea of throwing your helicopter around.

If you do get into trouble at this stage it is likely to take one of three forms:

(1) The model does not make it over the top of the loop and starts to fall inverted. This is why you started at a safe height. Hang on to the back stick and full power and the model should right itself.

(2) After completing three-quarters of a loop the model is reluctant to pull out of the ensuing dive. Here again, just hang on.

(3) When the loop is complete the model zooms wildly or comes to a stop in a nose high attitude. Be ready to push the stick forward as the model returns to level flight. You will probably need this anyway to re-establish forward flight.

When you are quite happy and confident with your untidy loops you can start to clean them up a little. This is where the 'idle up' switch on your transmitter starts to become very useful.

Now, once again at a safe height and with lots of forward speed, pull the stick back and as the model passes through the vertical climb position, reduce the pitch to zero. Keep the pitch at zero around the top half of the loop and then apply positive pitch as the model passes through the vertical dive position. By varying the back stick and the pitch you should eventually be able to achieve a true round loop. You will probably find it necessary to apply some negative pitch at the top of the loop to do this (Figure 96).

I did listen to advice on how to do a loop before my first

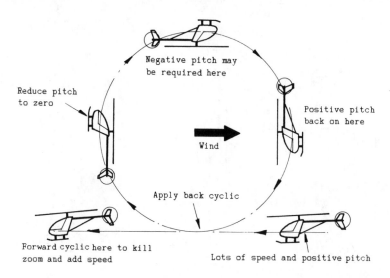

Fig. 96 Loop.

attempt at doing one with a *Kalt Baron 50*. After applying negative pitch at the top of the loop I was rewarded with the only inverted spiral dive I have ever seen by a helicopter! I applied full pitch and full power just too late to recover. So remember – get it round the loop first, then tidy it up later.

The roll

There is something rather incongruous about a helicopter performing a roll, yet given a suitable model, it is probably easier to do than a loop. It is certainly easier to produce a reasonable looking roll than it is to perform a truly round loop.

As with the loop, your first roll should be performed by climbing to a safe height, putting on lots of forward speed – it helps to do it downwind – and holding the lateral cyclic hard over until the roll is complete. The nose should be raised slightly just before starting the roll, but don't overdo it, since it will lose you too much of that precious forward speed.

Roll direction for best results depends on the model, but usually should be away from the forward going blade. This means rolling to the right with a clockwise main rotor or to the left if the rotor rotates anticlockwise.

Your first attempt will be untidy and probably more like a barrel roll (Figure 97), but don't worry too much about that at this stage.

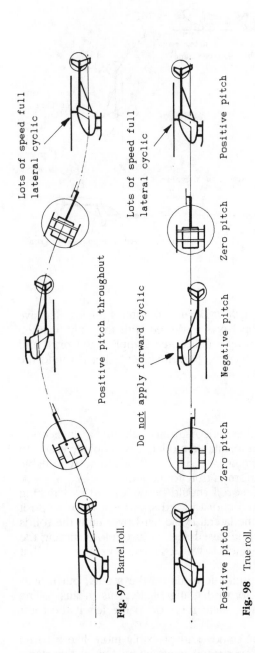

Lots of speed full
lateral cyclic

Positive pitch throughout

Fig. 97 Barrel roll.

Lots of speed full
lateral cyclic

Do _not_ apply forward cyclic

Positive pitch   Zero pitch   Negative pitch   Zero pitch   Positive pitch

Fig. 98 True roll.

Lots of speed full power and
full positive pitch nose down

Full positive pitch   Zero pitch   Full negative pitch nose down   Zero pitch   Positive pitch nose down
nose still down   apply aft cyclic if necessary

Fig. 99 Roll with nose down throughout.

134

If you get into trouble it will probably take one of the following forms:

(1) Roll rate is very slow. If the model only gets as far as being on its side and then starts to fall, apply opposite lateral cyclic to roll out and back stick to recover. Having got as far as the inverted stage, the easiest answer is pull the stick back and perform a half loop to recover (that's why you needed lots of height).

(2) The model reaches the inverted point and stops rolling. Apply back stick to half loop back to normal flight. Do it again to make sure you did not just let go of the stick in fright!

(3) All forward speed is lost before the roll is complete. Most models will probably complete the roll anyway, but some may begin to fall inverted, in which case use full back stick and pray! The answer to this one is more forward speed which means more power or a cleaner model. Don't be tempted to push the stick forward when inverted: this will kill speed very rapidly. It's much better to add a little up to drop the nose. When you become very proficient it is possible to coax an underpowered model through a roll, but we will come to that in a moment.

Having mastered the art of performing untidy, diving, barrelly rolls, we can start to improve them. This is where our old friend the 'idle up' switch comes in handy again. Start your roll as before and as the model approaches the inverted point, pull the throttle stick back to reduce the pitch to zero, or slightly negative. Don't overdo it at this stage. An inverted, climbing, helicopter tends to cause the brain and thumbs to go out of synch! As the model rolls from inverted to normal flight, move the throttle stick back to the normal position.

What you are aiming for is something like Figure 98 where pitch is reduced to around zero when the model is on its side, goes down to negative when inverted, back to zero when the helicopter is on its other side and finally back to normal. Keep practising until you can perform smooth, axial, rolls (?).

There is another approach to the problem of maintaining speed throughout the roll which is used by those of above average ability. Normally, at the entry to the roll, the model is in high speed forward flight which means that it is at full power and in a nose down attitude to prevent it climbing. If this attitude can be maintained throughout the roll, then the model will be continuously pulled forward by the main rotor. In order to keep this nose down

135

attitude during the inverted phase (Figure 99) we need to have as much negative pitch available as the normal positive figure – typically 6°-7°! Obviously, this large pitch range will make the model more difficult to fly in most other situations.

Combinations

Apart from one other ingredient, which we will discuss in a moment, all helicopter aerobatics consist of combinations of the loop and roll. Take for example the reversal, or split ess (Figure 100), consisting of a half roll followed by a half loop. Starting

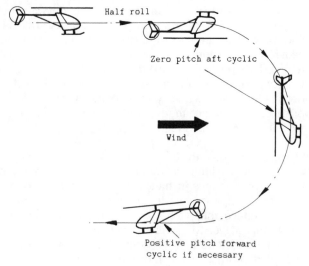

Fig. 100 Split-S.

downwind and with lots of speed, roll inverted and hold this for a moment (consult the judges of your particular contest for advice on how long a 'moment' is) with zero, or slight negative pitch. Complete the figure by pulling 'up' and adding positive pitch as the model passes through the vertical dive position. This one is easy to do but difficult to get right.

The other ingredient is the humble stall turn, which again is easy to do until you attempt to add lengthy periods of vertical climb or dive as required in contests. Under these conditions the pitch setting becomes very critical. If you simply leave the positive pitch

136

on the model will fall over backwards during the climb. This situation is made more complicated by the fact that there is no indication from the transmitter stick to tell you exactly where zero pitch is, so you have to fly by feel and observation of the model. This is what might be called 'flying by the seat of the retina'.

All of the points we have discussed so far can be combined in one manoeuvre, the rolling stall turn (Figure 101), originally known

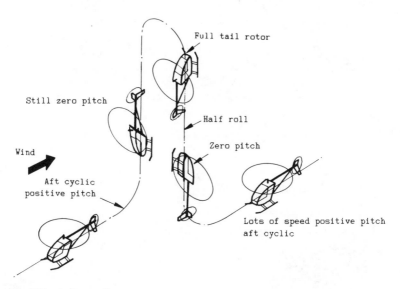

Fig. 101   Rolling stall turn.

as the Belgian stall turn. This commences with a quarter loop (back cyclic, positive pitch) followed by a vertical climb (neutral cyclic, zero pitch), a half roll (full lateral cyclic), a further vertical climb (if you are lucky), a stall turn (full rudder), a vertical dive back to the point where you started the climb (still zero pitch) and another quarter loop (back cyclic, positive pitch) to recover. What usually happens is that the model runs out of steam during the half roll and tumbles backwards. If the model has enough inertia to complete the roll its eventual path will depend on whether the initial climb was truly vertical and the pitch exactly zero.

The rolling stall turn is one of the most difficult manoeuvres and it should be apparent that it requires a clean, high powered helicopter. With a suitable model, it still requires considerable practice, however, to produce something recognisable. It is only possible to give a general description above on how to go about it, since every helicopter requires its own particular technique to produce the desired result. In particular, it is worth experimenting with the direction of both the roll and the stall turn to see if any improvement can be found.

Advanced aerobatics

Inverted flight

Some years ago, a model helicopter enthusiast in America decided that he would be the first to fly a model helicopter inverted. For nearly a year he practised flying his model with one of its controls reversed. Eventually he reached the point where he could mentally reverse the action of one or more controls and was then able to make a sustained inverted flight. The day after this first flight he learned that one month earlier someone in Europe had done the same thing by using a special transmitter with a switch which simultaneously reversed the fore/aft cyclic, collective pitch and tail rotor functions!

For a while after this 'technological leap' everyone was flying their helicopters inverted. The novelty soon wore off, however. Nowadays it is regarded very much as a 'party trick' and there are only a few helicopter radios which feature an 'invert' switch.

Assuming that you wish to become one of the select few and possess a suitable radio, you should set up the collective pitch travel in a manner which gives a mirror image of the normal travel when the invert switch is operated. If the normal travel is, say −3° to +7°, then the invert travel should be +3° to −7° (Figure 102).

Now all you have to do is to take the model up to a safe height, roll it inverted and flip the switch. Your model will now behave in a perfectly normal manner, but the other way up. Orientation can be a problem, however, so take it easy at first. In practice, you will probably find that less pitch is required since the rotor downwash is not hindered by the fuselage and is more efficient. For this reason the model also tends to be more stable inverted!

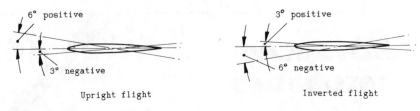

Fig. 102 Pitch offset for inverted flight.

In fact, it is quite possible to fly your model inverted for short periods without the use of an invert switch. If a lot of negative pitch is available, as previously described for aerobatics, the model may be rolled inverted and the throttle stick pulled hard back. Do it, as always, at a safe height and remember that the tail was the most difficult function to control initially and is the most likely one to give you problems when the action is the opposite of what you have come to expect. An inverted pirouetting helicopter can make even the most hardened flier turn into a quivering jelly!

Outside loops

Let's say straight away that these are not for the faint-hearted – or the poorly maintained helicopter. Nonetheless, they are possible, as several fliers have proved. Obviously you will need lots of negative pitch!

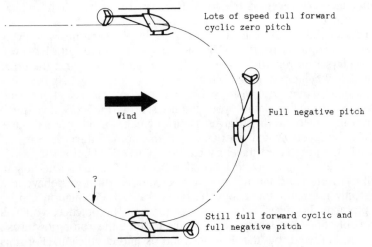

Fig. 103 Outside loops.

The 1986 Morley *MXA plus* is a fully aerobatic version of the *MXA* trainer, for .040-.045 cu.in. (6.6-7.5 cc) engines. Model in top picture has a tuned pipe exhaust which can be a mixed blessing in a helicopter.

Entry speed is a problem here. Too much speed will certainly be a hindrance to most – but not all – models. Start with the model travelling downwind and as high as possible. Push the collective stick full forward and, as the model passes through the vertical dive position, apply full negative pitch (Figure 103). If the model is reluctant to pull out into inverted flight, the best answer is to roll out and apply back cyclic and positive pitch to recover. The model should make it through the inverted position, but will lose lots of speed in the process, which can cause any number of effects during the inverted climb phase.

The best course of action here depends on just when the model actually stops:

(1) During the initial stages of the inverted climb the best solution is to apply back cyclic to drop the nose and then roll out.

(2) At the vertical climb position apply full rudder to produce a stall turn and recover by a quarter loop into normal flight.

(3) If the model makes it past the vertical climb, hang on to the full forward cyclic and apply full positive pitch.

It is worth pointing out at this stage that you will be setting up a situation where a tail boom strike is a distinct – and very spectacular – possibility!

Consecutive loops and rolls

There is a young man in Japan called Tatsui Ikobe who can perform rolling circles with his Kalt *Baron 60*. If you wish to know how he does it – please ask him, not the writer!

If you have a model which will perform round loops and axial rolls then it is quite capable of performing several loops or rolls consecutively. The limiting factor here is your ability to fly the model (a better word might be 'coax') through the manoeuvres without losing too much speed. This ability can only be acquired by constant practice and it goes without saying, perhaps, that you will damage models in the process.

However, one thing that is certain to hold you back in the learning process is a fear of breaking the model and you must conquer this or try something else.

This explains why most of today's top helicopter pilots are connected with the model trade in some way!

The sky's the limit

Only a few years ago it was a considerable achievement to fly a model helicopter at all. To be able to fly one around in a circuit made you one of the top fliers in the world. A loop was thought to be possible and there were those who claimed to have seen one.

The modern model helicopter has progressed to the point where learning to fly them is comparatively easy and loops and rolls are commonplace. Having reached that stage, from now on it really is up to you. It is possible to perform any manoeuvre with a helicopter that can be performed by a fixed wing aircraft. Several fliers have now demonstrated four point rolls and square loops, while there are rumours of inverted autorotations! Go to it.

See Appendix 5 for details of all aerobatic manoeuvres which can be performed in FAI contests.

17 Contests

Competition flying is fun!

The writer has been a confirmed competition flier for almost as long as he has been an aeromodeller and it is a source of amazement to him that many modellers do not appreciate the enjoyment which may be had from contest flying. It is not a question of being a 'pot hunter' since some of the most enjoyable events are those in which one finishes a resounding last.

Flying in a contest of any kind gives you some positive indication of your ability and of your rate of progress. Most activities are at their most enjoyable during the learning phase and contests put you into a situation where you learn more and have some means of assessing how much you have learnt.

Don't think in terms of winning, rather in terms of doing better than you did last time. If you are consistently being beaten by flier A, who always places one position from last, then make it your ambition to beat him and make him finish last. If you pursue this approach long enough, you may find yourself at the top of the list one day. Having got there, you will find it much harder to stay there – which is another learning process.

In an event where scores are given, try to score more points at each succeeding contest. Even if you continue to place last, you are making progress if your score improves each time. Competition flying is fun if you get your priorities right.

Novelty contests

There are many variations on the basic theme of a novelty, or fly-for-fun, contest. Participation in any of these will teach you a lot in

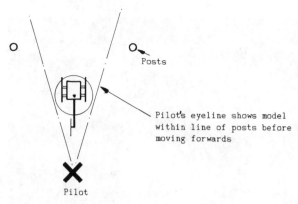

Fig. 104 Flying through gates.

terms of precision control of your model. Some of them can be potentially damaging to the model due to the need to fly between or under some kind of obstacle and many potential competitors are deterred by this.

The amount of risk involved, however, depends entirely on how hard you are trying and the risks are usually not too great if you think before you act and proceed with caution. Most of these events take the form of a race against the clock. If you regard the event purely as a learning process and ignore the time element, then you have much to learn. One very big advantage of this type of event is that you are normally allowed an unlimited number of attempts. It is surprising how the time taken to complete the course reduces after a number of tries.

A typical novelty contest will involve such things as flying through 'gates' formed by vertical posts (rather like a ski slalom), flying under paper tapes supported by poles, knocking down bottles – which may be filled with water to increase their weight – picking up items with the landing skids, or landing in small boxes.

Flying through gates is much easier if performed with a small helicopter, since the gates will normally be of a size suitable for a large model. Don't attempt to fly through any gate which you are viewing from the side. Follow the model round and ensure that you are standing facing the gate with the model hovering in front of it before attempting to fly through it (Figure 104). Normally, no marks will be scored if the model is higher than the pole tops.

Flying under paper tapes should be tackled in the same way as flying through gates. Obviously you must be lower than the tops of the poles to be under the tape. A common requirement is for the model to pass under the tape, back over the top of it and then

145

Scale models such as the Robbe *Ecureuil* can be just as aerobatic as any other model and the chunky fuselage can make orientation simpler. Given good mechanics and a good engine, performance is mainly a matter of correct setting up and pilot ability.

under it again. Hitting the tape usually causes no more damage than a loss of points, but hitting the poles can be very damaging so do be sure that the model is lined up on the gap before moving forwards.

Knocking down bottles can be surprisingly difficult, particularly if you are using a small model to make the gates easier! With an average sized model it is normally sufficient to hit the bottle with the landing skids while moving sideways. The best approach with a small model is to fly straight at the bottle and hit it head on with the model's nose. This also reduces the possibility of a heavy bottle tipping the model over.

Picking up items with the skids is the most difficult task, but it has the advantage of being the least likely to cause damage to the model. Usually the item to be picked up is a plywood pyramid with a hook on the top (Figure 105). The dimensions of this particular device were established many years ago by Dieter Schlüter, the father of radio-controlled helicopter flying. In most cases the flier is allowed to place the pyramids in any position he wishes and he should take advantage of this to position the hooks in such a way

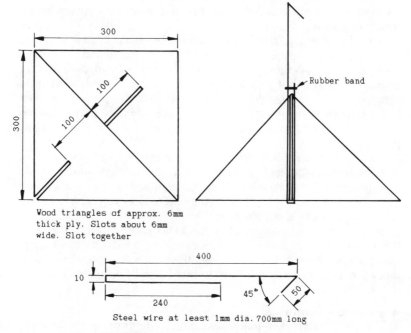

Wood triangles of approx. 6mm thick ply. Slots about 6mm wide. Slot together

Steel wire at least 1mm dia. 700mm long

Fig. 105 Pyramid for lifting with landing skids.

147

that the model may be hovered alongside with its nose into wind and the hooks orientated towards the skids. By practising this you will almost certainly find that one particular side is easier than the other. Having established the model in a stable hover alongside the hook it is merely (?) a question of moving the model sideways to engage the hook and then climbing away. Releasing the object can sometimes be a problem, but 'bumping' the model onto the ground and away again usually does the trick.

Landing in small boxes is not quite as hazardous as it sounds since the 'box' is normally enclosed by lines drawn on the ground. This is merely a matter of practice, but do beware of dumping the model down hard in the heat of the moment and causing a tailboom strike by the rotor blades.

Scale contests

There are no internationally established rules for scale helicopters as yet and there are, therefore, several sets of national, or even local, rules in use. Scale judging standards are very variable and many contests are won by models which bear little resemblance to the full-size machine other than in the shape of the fuselage.

It is, for example, fairly common to find that the tail rotor is on the wrong side of the fuselage, or that the main rotor rotates in the wrong direction.

Many full-size machines have multi-bladed main rotors, yet there are few attempts made to duplicate these in the model. The more enterprising competitor will have a multi-blade head available for display purposes, but this will be replaced by a two-bladed head (complete with non-scale stabiliser bar) for flying. This is then explained away by pointing out that scale models of fixed wing machines are allowed to change the propeller for flying without any points penalty!

Very few, if any, helicopter scale contests feature the kind of meticulous measuring and checking of the models which would accompany a similar contest for conventional models. This situation is propagated by the fact that there are very few accurate scale drawings of helicopters available.

As a result scale competitions for helicopters usually become a flying contest for semi-scale models. This tends to discourage participation by all but the best fliers. It also prevents many modellers from taking the trouble to build a really accurate model.

Autorotation contests

These are a fairly new innovation which are proving to be great fun. All competitors are given just one attempt at performing a spot landing from an autorotation in which the motor must be stopped. The winner is the closest to the spot, the distance being measured from the mainshaft of the model.

FAI aerobatic contests

Contests held to the International Rules (category F3C) established by the Federation Aeronautique International (FAI) received a considerable boost when the event was raised to World Championship status, the first World Championships being held in Canada in 1985.

This event is now considered to be the number one event for helicopters throughout the world but needs considerable practice – and dedication – to be really competitive. Unfortunately, most countries only recognise this event and do little to encourage the newcomer. The U.S.A. is much more enlightened in these matters and organises a series of events which are split into novice, intermediate and expert classes in addition to the FAI event. These are further subdivided into junior and senior classes which gives even more encouragement. It does, however, seem unlikely that juniors outside the U.S.A. can afford to fly R/C helicopters!

As with other contests, you do not need to be highly competitive to fly in the FAI class. It is even possible to compete without being capable of performing all of the required manoeuvres. Neither is it necessary to select manoeuvres which have high scoring potential, or 'K' factor. This only becomes necessary when you stand some chance of winning.

Competitors fly, one at a time, before a set of judges who give a score for each manoeuvre (maximum 10). This score is then multiplied by a difficulty – or 'K' – factor to give the actual score.

The competitor starts his motor in a 'ready box' and then proceeds to the 'helipad' where he flies his model through three compulsory hovering manoeuvres, landing after each one. He then has a choice of four more manoeuvres which he selects from a list of fourteen which include both hovering and aerobatic options. These have different 'K' factors according to their difficulty.

Finally, the model must perform either an engine off auto-rotation (K=9) or a powered landing (K=6) onto the centre of the helipad.

See Appendix 5 for full details and rules of the FAI F3C class event.

18 Conclusions

Is it worth it?

The hobby/sport of flying R/C model helicopters requires great persistence and perseverance to fully master it. However, the results are very rewarding and well worth the effort. Modern designs and equipment make the task much easier than it used to be and have brought about a great increase in the number of successful fliers. If they can do it, so can you.

Finally, at the risk of being repetitive, a few dos and don'ts:

Do

Seek experienced help – preferably before beginning construction of your model.

Buy from a specialist shop which offers a setting-up service and, if possible, flying tuition.

Use a tail rotor gyrostabiliser.

Start with a non-scale pod and boom type.

Remember that a model helicopter can be a dangerous device and treat it with respect.

Realise that uninformed spectators may not be aware of the model's capacity for injury and proceed accordingly.

If you must 'go-it-alone', read everything you can obtain on the subject first.

Fly with care.

Don't

Fly without adequate insurance.

Take risks involving other people or their property.

Repair broken rotor blades.

Try to salvage and re-use damaged components which you are not absolutely sure of.

Use weighted blades until you are absolutely sure that you need them.

Try to walk before you can crawl!

And finally:

Welcome to a fascinating and thoroughly habit-forming hobby. Good luck!

Appendix 1
Helicopters

Manufacturer	Model	Motor size	Type	Remarks
GMP	Cricket	0.25 – 0.28 cu.in.	Pod & boom	Fixed pitch
	Cobra	0.40 – 0.50 cu.in.	Pod & boom Aerobatic	
	Competitor	0.50 – 0.61 cu.in.	Pod & boom Aerobatic	
	Stork Special Edition	0.61 cu.in.	Pod & boom Aerobatic	

A 'Jet Ranger' fuselage is available to fit the Cobra

Manufacturer	Model	Motor size	Type	Remarks
Graupner	Helimax 40	0.40 – 0.50 cu.in.	Pod & boom	
	Helimax 60/80	0.60 – 0.61 cu.in. or 0.80 – 0.90 cu.in. 4 stroke	Pod & boom Aerobatic	
	Hughes 500E	0.60 – 0.61 cu.in.	Scale	Helimax mechanics

An optional tail fairing is available for the Helimax 40 and 60/80

Manufacturer	Model	Motor size	Type	Remarks
Heim	Star-Ranger		Semi-scale Aerobatic	
	Bell 222	0.60 – 0.61 cu.in.	Scale with retracts	
	Star-Trainer		Trainer/ Aerobatic	
	Lockheed 286h		Semi-scale Aerobatic	
Hirobo	Shuttle	0.28 cu.in.	Pod & boom *Ready-to-fly* with motor	Mainly plastic
	Super Shuttle	0.32 cu.in.	Uprated Shuttle with cone start motor	
	Falcon 555	0.40 – 0.50 cu.in	Pod & boom	
	Falcon 888	0.60 – 0.61 cu.in.	Pod & boom	
	Stork	0.46 cu.in.	Pod & boom	Motor included
	Eagle	0.61 cu.in.	Pod & boom	
	Bell 'Jet Ranger'	0.60 – 0.61 cu.in.	Scale	
	Bell UH-1B 'Iroquois'	0.60 – 0.61 cu.in.	Scale	
	Bell UH-1B 'Iroquois'	22 cc petrol engine	Scale	Motor included
	Aerospatiale 'Gazelle'	0.60 – 0.61 cu.in.	Scale	
	Aerospatiale 'Lama'	0.60 – 0.61 cu.in.	Scale	
	Bell 47G-2	22 cc petrol engine	Scale	Motor included

The German firm of Peka-Luftechnik produces a range of 3, 4 and 5 bladed rotor heads with few moving parts. Development work is continual and a completely bearingless head is now available.

Manufacturer	Model	Motor size	Type	Remarks
	DDF—SST Series – Dual Damping Flapping Head			
	Agusta 109A	0.60 – 0.61 cu.in.	Scale	
	Jet Ranger	0.60 – 0.61 cu.in	Scale	
	Corvette	0.60 – 0.61 cu.in.	Freelance fuselage	
Ishipla	Chopper I	0.40 – 0.50 cu.in.	Pod & boom	Fixed pitch
	Chopper II	0.40 – 0.50 cu.in.	Pod & boom	
Kalt	Baron 20	0.20 – 0.28 cu.in.	Pod & boom	
	Baron 20MX	0.28 – 0.32 cu.in.	Uprated Baron 20	
	Baron 50	0.45 – 0.50 cu.in.	Pod & boom	
	Custom Baron 50	0.50 cu.in.	Pod & boom Aerobatic	
	Baron 60	0.60 – 0.61 cu.in.	Pod & boom Aerobatic	
	GS Baron	22 cc petrol engine	Pod & boom	Motor included
	FC Baron	0.80 – 0.90 cu.in. 4 stroke	Pod & boom	
	Bell 222	0.60 cu.in.	Scale	
	Ecureuil	0.60 – 0.61 cu.in.	Scale	
	Huey Cobra 500	0.50 – 0.60 cu.in.	Scale	
	Hughes 500	0.50 – 0.60 cu.in.	Scale	

Manufacturer	Model	Motor size	Type	Remarks
	Jetranger 500	0.50 – 0.60 cu.in.	Scale	
	Cyclone	0.40 – 0.50 cu.in.	Pod & boom	All plastic
	Omega	0.61 cu.in.	Pod & boom Aerobatic	

Bell 'Jet Ranger', 'Longranger' and '222' bodies are available to fit Baron 50 & 60 mechanics. A wider range of fuselages is available from the English importer.

Manufacturer	Model	Motor size	Type	Remarks
Kavan	Jet Ranger	0.61 cu.in.	Scale	
	Ranger	0.61 cu.in.	Semi-scale Trainer	Metal body
	Lockheed 286L	0.61 cu.in.	Scale	Retracting under-carriage
	Shark 40	0.40 cu.in.	Pod & boom Trainer	
KKK	Robinson R22HP	0.50 – 0.61 cu.in	Scale	Flybarless
	Robinson R22HP	20 cc petrol engine	Scale	Flybarless engine included
	Hughes 300	20 cc Petrol engine	Scale	
	Fox	0.50 – 0.61 cu.in.	Pod & boom Aerobatic	
MFA	Hughes 500D	0.40 cu.in.	Scale	Fixed pitch
	Sport 500	0.40 cu.in.		Fixed pitch
Micro-Mold	Lark 2—25	0.25 cu.in.	Pod & boom	Fixed pitch
	Lark 2—40	0.40 cu.in.	Pod & boom	Fixed pitch
Miniature Aircraft USA	X–Cell	0.61 cu.in.	Pod & boom Aerobatic	

Manufacturer	Model	Motor size	Type	Remarks
Morley	Bell 47	0.40 cu.in.	Semi-scale	
	Hughes 300	0.28 – 0.40 cu.in.	Scale	Mainly plastic
	Agusta 109	0.40 – 0.45 cu.in.	Scale with retracts	
	MXA	0.40 – 0.45 cu.in.	Pod & boom Trainer	
	MXA Plus	0.40 – 0.45 cu.in.	Pod & boom Aerobatic	
Robbe	Ecureuil	0.61 cu.in.	Scale Aerobatic	
	Avantgarde	0.61 cu.in.	Pod & boom Trainer	
	Clou	0.61 cu.in.	Pod & boom Aerobatic	Special radio needed
Schlüter	Mini Boy	0.40 – 0.60 cu.in.	Pod & boom Trainer	
	Heli-Star	0.61 cu.in.	Pod & boom Aerobatic	
	Superior	0.61 cu.in.	Pod & boom Aerobatic	
	Champion	0.61 cu.in.	Pod & boom Aerobatic	
	Junior 50	0.50 cu.in.	Pod & boom Aerobatic	
	Scout 60	0.61 cu.in.	Pod & boom Aerobatic	

A range of fuselages is available for the Heli-Star and Champion. These will not fit the Superior without considerable modifications. 3 and 4 bladed rotor heads are also available.

Accessories

Peka-Lufttechnik, Aachen are producing a range of 3, 4 and 5 bladed rotor heads of bearingless construction.

Slough R/C Models produce a Jet Ranger fuselage for the *Kalt* Baron 20 and a large range of fuselages for the Baron 50/60 models.

TSK, Tokyo produce a wide range of products aimed at improving the *Kalt* range.

Appendix 2
Helicopter motors

Manufacturer	Model	Capacity cu.in./cc	Special features
Enya	25 XH	0.25/4.1	
	SS 30 BB Heli	0.29/5.0	
	49XH	0.49/8.2	
	60 II XH	0.60/10.0	
HB	61 Stamo	0.61/10.0	
Kalt	GS 22	1.32/22.0	Petrol engine
OS	MAX 28 FSR—H	0.28/4.6	Dykes ring piston
	MAX 32 FSR—H	0.32/5.3	Dykes ring piston Also available with rear cone start
	MAX 45 FSR—H	0.45/7.5	Ringed piston
	MAX 50 FSR—H	0.50/8.3	Dykes ringed piston
	MAX 61 VF—H	0.61/10.0	Rear exhaust, ringed piston
	MAX 61 VF—H ABC	0.61/10.0	Rear exhaust, ABC piston/liner

Manufacturer	Model	Capacity cu.in./cc	Special features
	MAX 61 FSR—H	0.61/10.0	Ringed piston
	MAX 61 FSR—H ABC	0.61/10.0	ABC piston/liner
See Figure 106 for dimensions			
Rossi	61 Heli	0.61/10.0	Front exhaust, rear intake motor specifically designed for *Heim* mechanics
Schlüter	SHC 10 Ring	0.61/10.0	Modified by *Schlüter* from *Webra* 61 RCH, ringed piston
	SHC 10 ABC	0.61/10.0	As above, ABC piston/liner
Super Tigre	S29H ABC/R	0.29/5.0	
	S45H ABC/R	0.45/7.5	ABC piston/liner
	S61H ABC/R	0.61/10.0	with ringed piston
	S90H ABC/R	0.90/14.8	
Webra	61 RCH	0.61/10.0	

Motor	Disp. (cc)	Bore (mm)	Stroke (mm)	Output (PS or BHP/rpm)	Practical range (rpm)
MAX.61FSR-HABC	9.95	24.0	22.0	1.7/16,000	2,000~16,000
MAX.61FSR-H	9.95	24.0	22.0	1.7/16,000	2,000~16,000
MAX.61VF-HABC	9.95	24.0	22.0	1.7/16,000	2,000~16,000
MAX.61VF-H	9.95	24.0	22.0	1.7/16,000	2,000~16,000
MAX.50FSR-H	8.27	22.4	21.0	1.45/15,000	2,000~16,000
MAX.45FSR-H	7.47	21.8	20.0	1.3/16,000	2,000~16,000
MAX.28F-H	4.57	18.5	17.0	0.9/16,000	2,000~17,000

159

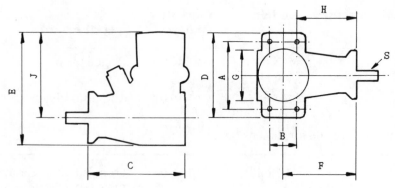

Fig. 106 OS helicopter motor dimensions.

O.S. Helicopter engines

				Mounting dimensions (mm)						Weight (g)
A	B	C	D	E	F	G	H	J	S	
52	25	96	60	100	66	42	53.5	78.5	UNF$\frac{1}{4}$-28	565
52	25	96	60	100	66	42	53.5	78.5	UNF$\frac{1}{4}$-28	565
52	25	96	61	101	66	42	53.5	79.7	UNF$\frac{1}{4}$-28	580
52	25	96	61	101	66	42	53.5	79.7	UNF$\frac{1}{4}$-28	580
45	21	88	55	92	63	36.4	52.5	73.5	UNF$\frac{1}{4}$-28	410
42	17.5	85	50	83	60.3	32.6	51.6	66.3	UNF$\frac{1}{4}$-28	335
38	15	75	45	75.5	53	29	45.5	60.7	UNF$\frac{1}{4}$-28	250

Appendix 3
Helicopter radios

Manufacturer	Model	No. of channels	PCM/PPM	Special features
Circus Hobbies	Cirrus	7	PPM	Special *JR* built system with 3 axis stick (Mode 3)
Fleet	XP/FM Heli 7	7	PPM	
	PCM—7HF	7	PCM/PPM	Combined heli/fixed wing set
Futaba	Challenger 5NH	5	PPM	
	Gold Series 7FGH	7	PPM	Invert switch
	8HP	8	PCM	
	8SGHP	8	PCM	Clock/timer and Tachometer
	1024 PCM	8	PCM/PPM	Programmable for 6 models

Graupner produce several modular R/C systems which can be set up for use with helicopters

Manufacturer	Model	No. of channels	PCM/PPM	Special features
JR	Core 5	5	PPM	
	Core 7	7	PPM	
	Apex	7	PPM	
	PCM 9	9	PCM	
	Apex Computer	8	PCM/PPM	Programmable for up to 7 models

Multiplex produce several modular R/C systems which can be set up for use with helicopters. The 'Royal mc' set has several different helicopter modules available, including modules with a memory for memorising trim settings, etc.

Robbe produce several modular R/C systems which can be set up for use with helicopters

Sanwa	DB Laser 7H	7	PPM	

Simprop produce several modular R/C systems which can be set up for use with helicopters

Sprengbrook several of the Multiplex R/C systems are sold under this label

Appendix 4
Gyros

Manufacturer	Model	No. of units	Separate battery	Special features
Fleet	F—340	3	Yes	Switched gain
Futaba	FP—G132	3	Optional	Switched gain
	FP—G152	3	Optional	As above but different connectors
	FP—G154	2	No	Budget system
Graupner	NEJ—110	2	No	*JR* unit
JR	NEJ—110	2	No	Variable gain
KO		2	No	Gain not setable from transmitter
Morley		1	No	Stick preferential
Multiplex		2	No	*KO* unit
Quest		1	No	Variable gain

Manufacturer	Model	No. of units	Separate battery	Special features
Robbe	Autopilot	3	No	*Futaba* unit
Sanwa		3	Yes	Switched gain
WMP		2	No	Variable gain

Appendix 5
FAI Schedule

5.4. CLASS F3C HELICOPTER
General Rules valid from 1/1/88. (For General Rules see also Sporting Code 1.4.15.)

5.4.1. **Definition of a Radio Controlled Helicopter**
A helicopter is a heavier-than-air aeromodel which derives all of its lift and horizontal propulsion from a power driven rotor system(s) rotating about a nominally vertical axis (or axes). Fixed horizontal supporting surfaces up to 4% of the swept area of the lifting rotor(s) are permitted. Ground effect machines (hovercraft), convertiplanes or aircraft that hover by means of propeller slipstream(s) deflected downward are not considered to be helicopters.

5.4.2. **Prefabrication of the Model**
Permitted: A helicopter which is assembled by the builder from prefabricated parts and in which the builder installs the equipment.

5.4.3. **General Characteristics**
Area: Maximum swept area of the lifting rotor(s) counting only once any area of superposition cannot exceed 300 dm². For twin rotor helicopters whose rotors are farther than one rotor radius apart the total swept area of both rotors must not exceed 300 dm².

Weight: Maximum 6 kg without fuel.

Motor: Piston motor displacement, maximum 10 cm³. Electric or elastic motors, no restrictions.

Tail Gyro: An electronic rate gyro is permitted on the yaw axis only.

Rotor Blades: All-metal main or tail rotor blades are forbidden.

Contest Site: Figure 5.4 contains the contest site plan. (*See Fig. 107, below.*)

5.4.4.
(a) **Number of Helpers**

Each competitor is allowed only one mechanic/caller. The mechanic/caller can not act as coach but can only announce

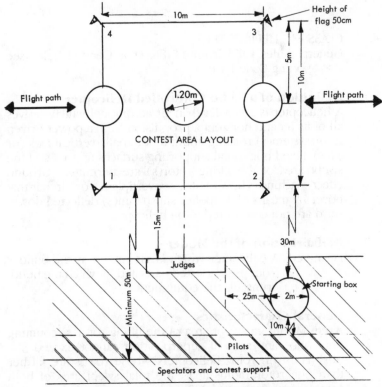

(1) For each manoeuvre, where the pilot must occupy a helipad, he can choose between one of the two outer helipads.

(2) PROHIBITED AREA Pilots overflying this area will be penalized by scoring zero points for the current flight.

(3) Helipads must be marked in such a manner so as not to interfere with the landings. Chalk or paint is recommended. Platforms that result in an obtrusive edge are not recommended.

Fig. 107 Helicopter contest area.

The prototype of the original Kalt *Baron 60*. This manufacturer produces a dozen or so different models and various fuselages are available to suit several of them.

the start and finish of each manoeuvre. Team managers cannot help the competitor at the starting box. Team managers can observe the flight from a position 5 metres behind the judges and away from the starting box. Team managers can be substituted if there is no mechanic/caller.

(b) **Number of Models**
The number of models eligible for entry is only two (2). The competitor is allowed to change the model as long as the primary model is still in the starting box.

5.4.5. **Number of Flights**
At Continental and World Championships, each competitor is entitled to four (4) official flights. At open national or international contests this number is not mandatory.

5.4.6. **Definition of an Official Flight**
There is an official flight when the competitor is officially called, whatever the result. The flight may be repeated, at the Contest Director's discretion when for any unforeseen reason, outside the control of the competitor, the model fails to make a start such as:

(a) The take-off cannot be made within the allowed time limit due to safety reasons.
(b) The competitor can prove that the take-off was hindered by interference from outside.
(c) Judging was impossible for reasons outside the control of the competitor. (Model, engine, or radio failures are not considered outside the control of the competitor.)

In such cases the flight may be repeated immediately after the attempt, during the same round or at the end of the round, at the discretion of the Contest Director.

5.4.7. **Marking**
Each manoeuvre is given a score between 0 and 10 (including half points) by each judge. Any manoeuvre not completed shall be scored zero (0) points. The manoeuvres flown away from the 10 metre square must be performed in an airspace which will allow them to be clearly seen by the judges. This airspace is defined to lie between 0 and 60 degrees vertically and 0 and 90 degrees horizontally. The non-observance of this rule will be penalized by a loss of points. There shall be an official located in a position where any flight over the prohibited area (see Fig. 107) can be observed. A visual or audible signal shall be given to

168

indicate such overflights. Competitors over-flying this area will be penalized by scoring zero (0) points for the current flight. In addition, there shall be no score when:

(a) The competitor flies a model than has been flown in the same contest by another competitor, or flies a model that does not comply with the definition and general characteristics of a radio controlled helicopter.
(b) The competitor fails to start his model in the pre-scribed starting sequence.
(c) The competitor does not deliver his transmitter to the impound or operates his transmitter during a round without permission.
(d) The competitor does not release his model at the pre-scribed starting box or receives assistance from more than one helper.
(e) The competitor gets his transmitter from the impound before he is officially called.
(f) The competitor switches on his transmitter before the signal to start his engine and adjust the model.
(g) The competitor enters the starting box before the final call.

5.4.8. **Classification**
The final classification will be determined by the sum of all flight scores except the lowest one which will be deleted. However, if only one round has been completed, the final classification will be obtained by this single round. In case of a tie for any of the first three places, the final result will be established by a fly-off and the final standing will be determined by the scores of the fly-off only.

5.4.9. **Judging**
(a) At Continental and World Championships the organiser must appoint a panel of five judges for each round. The final score of each flight is obtained by deleting the highest and lowest score for each manoeuvre from the five judges. At other contests the number of judges can be reduced to a minimum of three (3).
(b) There shall be training flights for judges with a briefing immediately before and after a World Championship.
(c) The scoring system must be organised in such a way that the pilots and the spectators can clearly see the scores awarded by all judges for each manoeuvre.

5.4.10. **Organisation**

(a) For transmitter, frequency control and starting order see Sporting Code, paragraph 2.5.6k.

(b) Preparation time:
The competitor must be called *at least 5 minutes* before he is required to enter the starting box. (For starting box layout see Fig. 107.) A starting box 2 metres in diameter, will be provided away from the flight line, spectators, competitors and models. When the timekeeper with the permission of the flight line director gives the signal to start the engine, the competitor is given 5 minutes to start his engine and make last minute adjustments. The model can only be hovered in the starting box up to eye level. The competitor in the starting box must reduce his engine's speed to an idle when the preceding competitor is about to execute the autorotation manoeuvre. The preparation time ends when the flight time begins.

(c) Flight time:
The flight time of 10 minutes begins when the competitor *leaves* the starting box with the permission of the judges. If the competitor is not ready after the 5 minute preparation time, he is allowed to complete his adjustments in the starting box; however, his flight time will have started at the end of the 5 minutes.

(d) Restrictions:
The competitor must fly his model directly without practising manoeuvres to the central helipad as soon as he leaves the starting box. After the competitor has left the starting box he is not allowed to touch the model, and if the motor stops, the flight is terminated.

5.4.11. **Schedule of Manoeuvres**

(a) Flight program:
The flight program consists of 9 compulsory manoeuvres. The competitor has 10 minutes to complete his flight program in *the following order*:

(1) Hovering M
(2) Horizontal Eight
(3) Nose-in Circle
(4) Top Hat
(5) 540° Stall Turn

Sophistication of the rotor head, electronics and control mechanisms is nowadays taken for granted and attention is being turned to improving the airframe and scale fidelity. This Morley Agusta 109 (.40 motors) comes complete with retractable undercarriage.

(6) Loop
(7) Roll
(8) Rolling Stall Turn
(9) Autorotation 180° Turn

If the allowed time expires before a manoeuvre is completed, that manoeuvre will be scored zero and the competitor is required to land his model as soon as possible. A new score sheet is issued for each contestant for each round. Only the contestant's number, not his name or nationality will appear on the score sheet. The manoeuvres are executed as described with landings performed only where listed.

(b) Performance of the Schedule:
No take-off or landing is allowed if it is not explicitly indicated in the manoeuvre descriptions. If a disallowed landing is made, the next manoeuvre will be scored zero (0). The manoeuvres should be performed in a smooth flowing sequence, preferably one manoeuvre should be performed on each pass before the judges. The competitor must execute each manoeuvre only once during one flight. No practice attempts are allowed. The name of each manoeuvre and its start and finish must be announced by the competitor or his helper. Unannounced manoeuvres will not be scored.

(c) Definition of eye level:
The rotor disc must be at an altitude corresponding to the level of the eyes of the competitor.

5.4.12. Description of Manoeuvres
During the hovering manoeuvres all the stops must be marked by 2 seconds duration. During all aerobatic manoeuvres the model maintains a safe height that corresponds with his particular requirements.

(1) Hovering M
Pilot stands on outer helipad, model takes off from central helipad and ascends vertically to eye level, hovers 2 seconds. With a constant heading the model moves along the diagonal line to the left or right corner, hovers 2 seconds. The model moves forward to the second corner, hovers 2 seconds and moves sideways to the third corner, hovers 2 seconds. The model moves backwards to the fourth corner, hovers 2 seconds and moves along the diagonal line to the

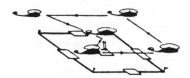

Fig. 108 Hovering M.

central helipad. The model hovers for 2 seconds over the central helipad and descends to a landing on the central helipad.

Downgrades:
(1) Model tilts, turns or moves horizontally during the manoeuvre.
(2) Model changes heading or speed during horizontal flight.
(3) Model goes off course or fails to hover over flags.
(4) Take off or landing is rough.
(5) Model does not land completely on the helipad.
(6) Pilot steps off the outer helipad.

(2) **Horizontal Eight**

Pilot chooses a location and must must not move from this spot during the manoeuvre. Model takes off from central helipad, ascends vertically to eye level and hovers 2 seconds, then starting forward begins a circle turning either right or left, maintaining longitudinal axis of model in alignment with flight path. The circle passes over the two flags on one side of the square and ends over the centre of the central helipad. Without slowing down, the model continues and makes a circle in the opposite direction, flies over the two other flags and returns to a point over the centre of the central helipad, hovers for 2 seconds and descends vertically to a landing on the central helipad.

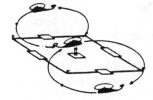

Fig. 109 Horizontal Eight.

Downgrades:
(1) The take off and/or landing is not smooth.
(2) Ascent or descent is not vertical.

(3) Model tilts, rotates or moves horizontally during ascent/descent.

(4) Model does not maintain constant speed and altitude during circles.

(5) Model's longitudinal axis is not in alignment with flight path.

(6) The circles are not round, equal size or do not pass directly over the flags.

(7) If the pilot moves from the chosen location during the manoeuvre the score will be zero.

(3) Nose-in Circle

Pilot stands on one of the outer helipads. The model takes off from the central helipad with nose pointed towards the pilot, ascends vertically to eye level and hovers for 2 seconds. The model then flies in a circular path to the left or right while maintaining a constant altitude and constant distance from the pilot. The nose must always point towards the pilot until the model returns to a point directly over the central helipad. The model hovers for 2 seconds and descends to a landing on the central helipad keeping the nose towards the pilot. The diameter of the circle is approximately 10 metres.

Downgrades:

(1) Take off and landing are rough and the heading changes.

(2) Altitude changes during circle. The radius is not constant and the nose of the model is not always pointed towards the pilot.

(3) The model did not land entirely on the helipad.

(4) The speed changes during the circle.

(5) The pilot steps off the outer helipad.

(4) Top Hat

The pilot stands at a fixed location chosen by him. The model flies at eye level 10 metres forward, straight and at a constant altitude. It hovers for 2 seconds vertically above the outer helipad and starts a vertical climb of 2 (two) metres. The model hovers 2 seconds, rotates slowly 360° to the left or the right about the yaw axis, hovers 2 seconds and climbs again for 2 metres. The model hovers for 2 seconds and moves forward for 10 metres until it is directly above the second outer helipad, hovers 2 seconds again. The model now descends 2 metres, hovers for 2 seconds and makes a slow 360° rotation about the yaw axis to the right or left, hovers 2 seconds, descends 2 metres vertically and hovers 2 seconds. The model flies again at eye level 10 metres forward straight and with a constant altitude. The direction of the 360° rotations during the ascent and descent must be *opposite* to each other.

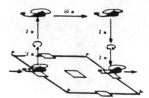

Fig. 110 Top Hat.

Downgrades:
(1) Model does not fly horizontally or vertically in the described parts.
(2) Altitude or lateral position changed during 360° rotations.
(3) Deviation in the vertical plane of the manoeuvre.
(4) Hover portions were not at prescribed locations.
(5) Rotations were not exactly 360° and not around yaw axis.
(6) The 360° rotations were performed at different altitudes.
(7) Rotations were not opposite direction and not centred over the helipads.
(8) The prescribed altitudes were not maintained.
(9) The pilot left the fixed location chosen by him.

(5) **540° Stall Turn**
The model flies straight and level for about 20 metres, then climbs vertically with a smoothly rounded curve of 90°. When the vertical climb stops, the model turns 540° around the yaw axis, so that the nose points downward. While diving, the model follows the same flight path as at the beginning

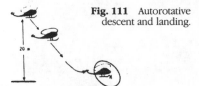

Fig. 111 Autorotative descent and landing.

The Kalt *Cyclone* makes extensive use of plastics and has a very short assembly time, typically one evening! For .50cu.in. motors.

of the manoeuvre. The radii of curves in climb and descent must be the same.

Downgrades:
(1) Model changed heading or altitude during horizontal flight.
(2) The pullup curve which brings the model in a vertical climb is too slow or too sudden.
(3) Ascent is not vertical.
(4) The model drifts laterally during the vertical climb or during the rotation.
(5) The model does not rotate exactly 540° and oscillates before the diving.
(6) The model finished the manoeuvre on a different flight path than it started on.
(7) The manoeuvre is not performed directly in front of the judges.

(6) **Loop**
The model flies straight and level for about 10 metres. It enters the loop while maintaining the longitudinal axis in the direction of flight. The model finishes the loop with the same heading and at the same altitude as at the beginning of the manoeuvre and exits the manoeuvre by flying straight and horizontal for a minimum of 10 metres.

Fig. 113   Loop.

Downgrades:
(1) The model oscillates, changes heading or altitude during the horizontal flight.
(2) The loop is not round.
(3) The model does not remain in the same plane.
(4) The finish of the loop ends on a different altitude or heading than the start.
(5) The speed is not constant.
(6) The loop is not performed in front of the judges.

(7) **Roll**
The model flies straight for about 10 metres. At a constant altitude the model starts a slow roll in either direction

Many helicopter manufacturers maintain display teams for demonstrations at Trade Shows. These two 'Baron 60 EX' models are flown by the British *Kalt* team. The nearer model, flown by Len Mount, has the space between the tailboom and the boomstay filled in for greater visibility. Other model, by John Wallington, has original type fuselage.

around an axis which coincides with the line of flight. It continues the roll in the same direction until it flies horizontally again and at a constant altitude for about 10 metres.

Scoring criteria: To get the maximum score the roll should be perfectly executed with a *minimum duration of 3 seconds.*

Fig. 114   Roll.

Downgrades:
(1) The model looses altitude during the roll.
(2) The model changes heading.
(3) The manoeuvre is not performed exactly in front of the judges.

(8) **Rolling Stall Turn**

The model flies straight and level for about 10 metres, then pulls up into a vertical ascent. During the vertical ascent the model performs a half axial roll. At the end of the ascent the model makes a 180° tail rotor turn followed by a vertical dive and pullout which brings the model back to the same altitude and heading as at the start of the manoeuvre. The manoeuvre is completed by flying straight and level for about 10 metres.

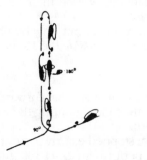

Fig. 115   Rolling stall turn.   **Fig. 116**   540° stall turn.

Downgrades:
(1) The model oscillates, changes heading or altitude during the horizontal flights.
(2) The pullup and pullout are not 90° exactly.
(3) The model does not ascend and descend vertically.

(4) The half roll is not in the axis of the vertical ascent.
(5) The half roll is not exactly 180° and the model oscillates before diving.
(6) The model does not exit the manoeuvre on the same heading and/or altitude as at the start of the manoeuvre.
(7) The manoeuvre is not performed exactly in front of the judges.

(9) **Autorotation with 180° Turn**

The model flies at a minimum altitude of approximately 20 metres and with a speed which requires less power than the stationary flight. When it reaches a position directly in front of the judges, the model must reduce the collective pitch to obtain the optimal autorotation. The engine must be stopped in front of the judges. The model performs a 180° turn and must land as close as possible to the centre of the central helipad.

Scoring criteria:

The maximum score of 10 points can only be obtained with a perfectly executed landing *inside* the central helipad.

A maximum score of 9 points can only be obtained with a perfectly executed landing *outside* the central helipad but the skids of the model must touch the central helipad.

A maximum score of 8 points can only be obtained with a perfectly executed landing *outside* the central helipad but *in* the 10 metre square.

A maximum score of 5 points can only be obtained with a perfectly executed landing *outside* the 10 metre square.

Downgrades:
(1) Brutal landing.
(2) The model lands while it still has forward speed.
(3) If the engine is still running during the manoeuvre, the score will be zero.
(4) The engine is not stopped exactly in front of the judges.
(5) Model does not perform an exact 180° turn.

Appendix 6
Useful addresses

Great Britain

Century Systems
111 Gretton Road
Winchcombe
Cheltenham
Gloucestershire
GL54 5EL

Dave Nieman Models
34 Watford Road
Sudbury
Wembley
Middlesex

Fleet Control Systems
47 Fleet Road
Fleet
Hampshire
GU13 8PJ

MacGregor Industries Ltd
Canal Estate
Langley
Berkshire
SL3 6EQ

MFA
The Mill
Mill Lane
Worth
Deal
Kent
CT14 0PA

Micro-Mold
Station Road
East Preston
West Sussex
BN16 5AG

Morley Helicopters Ltd
39 Prior Park Road
Bath
Avon
BA2 4NG

Quest Models
47/51 Waveney Road
Ipswich
Suffolk

Ripmax Models
Ripmax Corner
Green Street
Enfield
Middlesex
EN3 7SJ

Slough R/C Models
The Bishop Leisure Centre
Bath Road (A4)
Taplow
Berkshire

Sprengbrook
15a Victoria Road
Portslade
Sussex

Tigre Engines
Unit 10
Paramount Industrial Estate
Sandown Road
Watford
Hertfordshire

Watford Model Centre
103 St. Albans Road
Watford
Hertfordshire

Jack Williams Ltd
Eastwood
Beverly Road
Walkington
N. Humberside
HU17 8RP

United States of America

Ace R/C
116 W.19 ST.
P.O. Box 511EG
Higginsville
MO 64037

Airtronics Inc.
11 Autry, Irvine
CA 92718

American R/C Helicopters
635-11 N. Twin Oaks Valley Road
San Marcos
CA 92069

California Model Imports
P.O. Box 1695
Garden Grove
CA 92642

Circus Hobbies Inc.
3132 S. Highland Drive
Las Vegas
NV 89109

Condor Hobbies
17971 Sky Park Circle
Unit D, Irvine
CA 92714

Gorham Model Products
23961 Craftsman Road
Calabasas
CA 91302

Horizon Modelcraft
3812 W. Alabama
Houston
TX 77027

Kraft Systems Co.
450 West California Avenue
Vista
CA 92083

Miniature Aircraft Supply
and World Helicopters
2594 N. Orange Blossom Trail
Orlando
FL 32804

Yale Hobby Manufacturing Inc.
344 Main Street
Yalesville
CT 06492

Italy

OPS
Via Silvio Pallico 48
20052, Monza

Rossi Electronics & Bresciana s.r.l.
Via Corporalino, 5/7
25060 Cellatica (BS)

Super Tigre s.r.l.
Via Dell'Artigiano, 29
40065 Pianoro
Bologna

Japan

Enya Mfg.
553 Srai Machi
Nakanco-Ku
Tokyo

Futaba Denshi Kogyo Co. Ltd
Chiyoda-Ku
Tokyo

Hirobo Ltd
1-1-30 Hanazono-Cho
Kukuyama-Shi
Hiroshima Pref.
720

Kalt Sangyo Co. Ltd
1447-1 Higashi-Tanaka
Gotemba-Shi
Shizuoka Pref.

Kondo & Co. Ltd (KO)
No. 311 El Alcazar
Nishi-Nippori Building
29-11, Nishi-Nippori 6-Chome
Arakawa-Ku
Tokyo

O.S. Engines Mfg. Co. Ltd
6-15 3-Chome Imagawa
Higashisumiyoshi-Ku
Osaka, 546

Sanwa Electric Co. Ltd
7th Floor
Ohgimachi Park Building
3-6-26 Tenjinbashi
Kita-Ku, Osaka

World Creative Products & TSK
P.O. Box No. 34
Machida
Tokyo 194

Yamada Mfg Co. Ltd
Inuyama
Aichi
Japan

West Germany

Johannes Graupner
D-7312 Kirchheim/Tech.

Franz Kavan
Lindenaststrasse 56
D-8500 Nurnberg 10

Multiplex Modelltechnik GmbH
Neuer Weg 15
7532 Niefern

Peka-Lufttechnik Knipprath
Junkerstrasse 91
D-5100 Aachen

Robbe Modellsport GmbH
D-6424 Grebenhain 1

Schluter Modellbau
Dieselstrasse 5
6052 Muhlheim/Main

Simprop Electrical
4834 Harsewinkel
Ostude 7

Webra Modellbau GmbH
Industriestrasse 21
D-8588 Weidenberg

Index